Tim Duffy

COMMON FEATURES OF MICROSOFT® OFFICE 97®

ADDISON-WESLEY

An imprint of Addison Wesley Longman, Inc.

Reading, Massachusetts ▲ Menlo Park, California ▲ New York
Harlow, England ▲ Don Mills, Ontario ▲ Sydney ▲ Mexico City ▲ Madrid ▲ Amsterdam

Senior Editor: *Carol Crowell*
Project Manager: *Bess Deck*
Senior Production Supervisor: *Juliet Silveri*
Production Services: *Sue Purdy Pelosi*
Copyeditor: *Barbara Conway*
Proofreader: *Holly McLean-Aldis*
Technical Editor: *Dawn Remmel*
Indexers: *Mark Kmetzko, Bernice Eisen*
Page Checking: *MaryBeth Pitman, Cynthia Benn*
Compositor: *Compset Inc.*
Technical Art Consultant: *Joe Vetere*
Cover Design Supervisor: *Gina Hagen*
Text and cover design: *Linda Wade*
Marketing Manager: *Michelle Hudson*
Manufacturing Manager: *Hugh Crawford*

ISBN 0-201-32250-1

Addison-Wesley Publishing Company
Jacob Way
Reading, MA 01867
Web: http://www.awl.com/he/is/
Email: is@aw.com

1 2 3 4 5 6 7 8 9 10-DOW-00999897

To Wendy and Michael,
The two most important people in my life

PREFACE

Computer literacy is becoming a necessity in a world supercharged with information that is constantly evolving and updating. Millions of computers, both individually and in vast networks that span the globe, are constantly processing, analyzing, and organizing information. Advances in hardware and technology that once took decades, then years, now occur with startling frequency.

The challenge is real, it is identifiable, and it is immediate. What does one need to know to achieve and maintain both academic and business success in this technological maelstrom? For more than two decades, a professor at Illinois State University has been answering this question. His name is Tim Duffy, and he is both a teacher and a writer. As a teacher, he has taught introductory computer courses to thousands of his own students; as an author, he has introduced the very same computing concepts and skills to millions of students worldwide through his highly successful series.

In both his classes and his books, Duffy achieves a perfect balance between concept and skill, the why and the how, of computing. The why is the foundation of computing. Learn the concept and why that concept is important, and you can implement any skill. Because he teaches introductory computing throughout the school year, Duffy has intimate knowledge of exactly what conceptual information and what techniques students need and want to learn, and how to present enough of each to interest and challenge these active learners. Duffy knows what works in the classroom and what works in the computer labs. He knows where students can trip up, what assignments will make them think, what examples and exercises will illuminate the concepts, and what techniques will teach.

Duffy teaches what he writes and writes what he teaches. In his books, he brings his classroom teaching experience directly to you with the most innovative, up-to-date material available anywhere. His pedagogy is classroom tried and tested. There are completely new exercises and assignments, an all-new Windows 95-influenced design, and eye-popping graphics for today's visually oriented students. There are Internet and World Wide Web examples and active learning projects. The new Running Case sections are built around everyday problems that require both critical thinking and mastery of specific skills.

BUILDING KNOWLEDGE

For Duffy, learning is like building knowledge. A concept is presented, a feature or task is briefly described, and then students work with it. They complete an exercise or practice a task. Once that task is learned, they add a little more, building on what they are learning. After completing a small group of such tasks, each within its own context, students are presented with projects that unify the concepts and the skills. To achieve this natural balance between concepts and skills, there is constant reinforcement and evaluation throughout the book, including:

- **Active Learning.** Exercises apply software commands and features of each Office 97 application program to a specific problem, reinforcing skills described in the text.
- **Running Cases.** Everyday problems are presented with just enough information to challenge the students. The Running Case teaches critical thinking while reinforcing the basic skills that students have learned to that point.
- **Document to Web Presentation.** In-depth coverage shows students how to turn an ordinary document into a professional presentation, enhance its appearance, put it on the Web, and then improve the Web page to produce a professional electronic document.
- **Task Steps and Reference.** Reinforcing the Exercise sections provide students with summary information on how a task is performed to reinforce learning and to provide a reference for the future.
- **Self-Learning.** On Your Own boxes allow students to gain additional mastery of features as they explore Office 97 applications on their own.
- **Timely Tips.** Special notations tell students what potential traps they may encounter with a software tool, what can go wrong, and how to remedy the problem.
- **Toolbar Button Reference.** Tables of toolbar buttons give students a central location to find summaries of buttons found on frequently used toolbars.
- **Keyboard and Toolbar Icons.** Task-specific icons appear frequently in headings and tables to help students identify and remember keystrokes or toolbar buttons.
- **Self-Evaluation.** End-of-session exercises offer reinforcement in multiple formats: true/false, multiple choice, short answer, and project-based questions.
- **Unifying Features.** In *Office 97 Professional,* common features of Office 97 applications are covered first to give students the big picture of how to use an integrated suite.

Using Common Document-Related Commands 3–17

Save Command File, Save or [Save]

The Save command allows you to immediately save the active document. You may use the Save command periodically to save any changes that you have made in a document. You are generally encouraged to use some version of the Save command every 10 to 15 minutes or so to save your work to disk. Then, if the power goes out, all that you will have to redo is the work you've done since the last Save command.

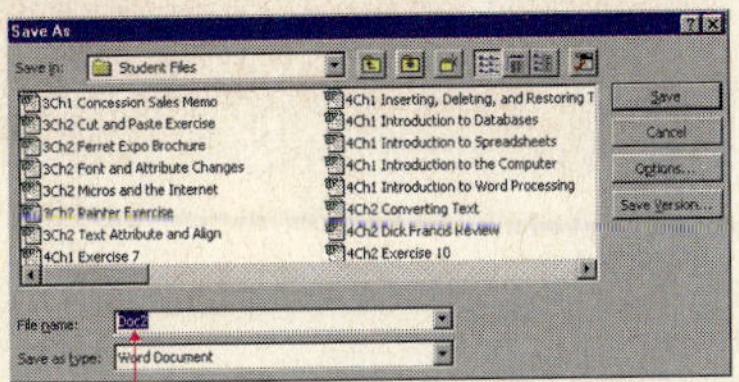

Figure 1.31
Using the Save As dialog box, you can save a document for the first time, change the name of a document, or store a document in a different location on the disk.

Providing Web Access to a File

Office applications permit you to save just about any document as an HTML file using the command sequence File, Save as HTML. It invokes the Save As HTML dialog box shown in Figure 1.33.

This feature allows you to create a document that you can retrieve directly using Internet Explorer. You can save a file as an HTML document on your local disk, or you can specify a URL to which you want the document saved.

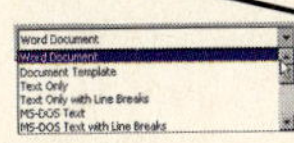

Figure 1.32
The available formats that Word can use to save a file to disk.

TIMELY TIP

Office has a built-in automatic save feature that you can use to restore some of your lost work. This AutoSave feature saves every 10 minutes or so. If you restart your computer after a power outage and then start the software application that you were using when you lost power, you will be stepped through the procedure of recovering the data. However you can recover only the data entered prior to the last AutoSave operation.

This feature can be activated by issuing the Tool, Options command sequence. When the Options dialog box opens, click the Save tab and examine the AutoRecover portion of the tab.

Duffy takes advantage of the **Web-aware tools** provided with Office 97 to help students translate their skills for use with the Internet and the Web.

Timely Tips inform students of helpful shortcuts, potential mistakes, or troubleshooting measures they can use with the text.

Using Common Document-Related Commands 3–5

graphic included in that box varies depending on the type of Office Assistant you choose. Figure 1.4 shows the default Office Assistant called Clippit.

Usually, the Office Assistant feature is activated when you start any Office Application. If it does not appear on your screen, you can activate it by clicking the Office Assistant button on the toolbar. Initially the Office Assistant appears something like Clippit shown in Figure 1.4. The appearance of the box changes, however, as you perform tasks within that application.

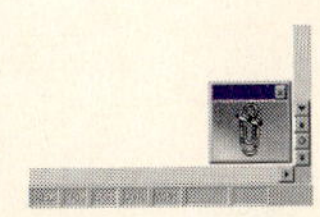

Figure 1.4
Clippit, the default Office Assistant.

If you perform a task that the Office Assistant thinks can be done more efficiently, it offers help without waiting for you to ask. A light bulb appears in the upper-right corner of the Office Assistant box (Figure 1.5). The appearance of the graphic changes, and a bubble displays a brief statement about the task you just performed. When you click an Office Assistant box with this appearance, the Office Assistant provides additional information on how you can make the task easier (Figure 1.6).

If you run into a problem and want the Office Assistant to help you, you can click the Office Assistant box to get its attention. The Office Assistant should look like that shown in Figure 1.7. If, for example, you want information about printing, you type the word *printing* in the box and then click the Search button. A list of topics appears, as shown in Figure 1.8. You can click on any topic to receive further information.

Information about the Print a document option appears in Figure 1.9. As you can see, this option generates a list of printing-related topics. Choosing the Print a range of pages option results in the Help screen shown in Figure 1.10.

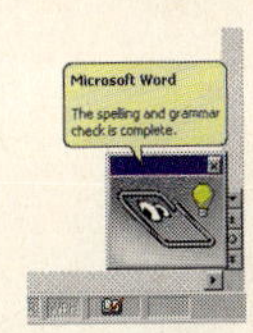

Figure 1.5
The Office Assistant offering to help you with the task of checking spelling.

You can change the type of Office Assistant from the default of Clippit to one of about eight other versions Office provides. When you right-click on the Office Assistant box, a context menu appears. Click the Options menu item to open the Office Assistant dialog box. Click the Gallery tab, and your screen should appear similar to the one shown in Figure 1.11. Follow the instructions given in the dialog box to examine the various Office Assistants and make your selection.

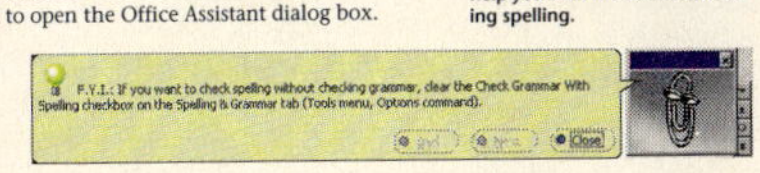

Figure 1.6
Additional information provided by the Office Assistant on using Word's spelling checker efficiently.

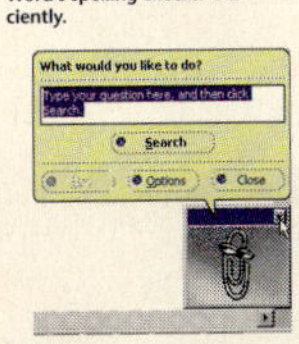

Figure 1.7
The Office Assistant ready to help you.

TIMELY TIP

If you have a sound system hooked to your computer, you can hear the Office Assistant making various sounds as you enter an Office document or perform tasks on a document.

Shortcut Icons

Check to see if your screen displays shortcut icons like those shown in Figure 1.1. Such shortcut icons may have been placed on your desktop screen by your school computer lab administrator. You can double-click one of these icons to start the application it represents. Notice that shortcut icons have a curved arrow embedded in a square to indicate that they are indeed shortcuts.

Using the Start Button

The menus invoked by clicking the Start button can also be used to start an Office application program. You first click the Start button to activate the Start menu, and then you point to Programs to activate that menu.

The next action you take depends on what appears on the Programs menu. If single application programs are listed, as shown in Figure 1.2, then you can click the desired program and a window will open for that application. If a Microsoft Office option appears on the Programs menu, click that, and then click the desired application when the menu for Office appears.

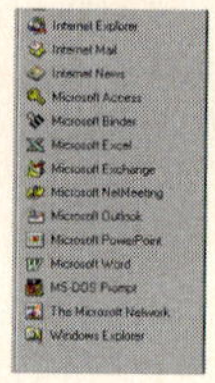

Figure 1.2
A list of Office-related programs displayed in the Programs menu invoked using the Start, Programs command sequence.

On Your Own

Your version of Microsoft Office may include a **shortcut bar** (Figure 1.1), which is a long, narrow bar that appears at the top of the screen. The shortcut bar allows you to quickly access existing documents or create new ones. It also provides direct access to the Schedule+ or Outlook feature (not covered in this text), as well as methods for accessing the Help feature or additional information that might be stored on a CD.

Using an Associated Document

As discussed in Session 2 of the Windows module, you can start an application by double-clicking the icon for an associated document. You can see associated documents when you are viewing the contents of a disk or folder using the My Computer window (Figure 1.3). If the icon for the associated document has an *X*, Excel starts and the document is loaded. If the icon has a *W*, Microsoft Word starts and the document is loaded. (Review Session 2 of the Windows module if you have any questions about other associated document icons.)

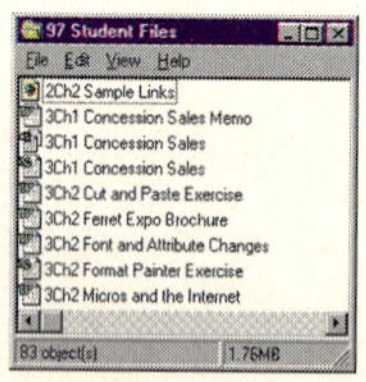

Figure 1.3
The 97 Student Files folder window with files shown for the Internet Explorer, Word, Excel, and the Binder.

USING THE OFFICE ASSISTANT

Every Office application provides help through a feature called the **Office Assistant**. There are several types of Office Assistants available. All appear as a box in the lower-right corner of the screen, and the

On Your Own boxes encourage students to explore the full range of features available in Office 97 applications.

Hands-On Exercises, based on the Running Case, give step-by-step instructions for learning each application. Numerous screen captures and button icons show students exactly what they need to know.

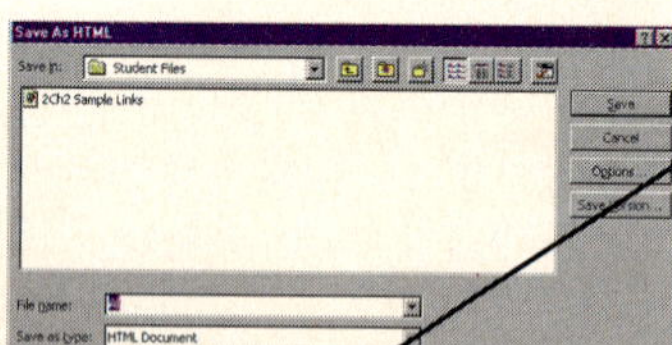

Figure 1.33
The Save As HTML dialog box allows you to create a file that can be accessed using a Web Browser like Internet Explorer.

Hands-On Exercise: Using File Commands

Isabel wants to examine several of the file-oriented commands that are found in various Office applications.

1. **Start Word.**

Start	Click to open the Start menu.
Programs	Click to open the Programs menu. If your computer has an Office 97 option, click that option.
Microsoft Word	Click to start Word. You should see a screen like that shown in Figure 1.34.

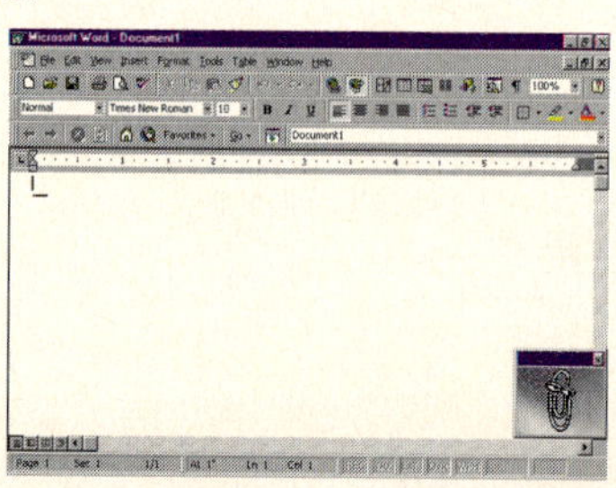

Figure 1.34
The Word application window.

2. **Open two documents using the Open button on the toolbar.**

Click to open the Open dialog box. Make the necessary changes to access the disk or folder containing the student files used with this textbook.

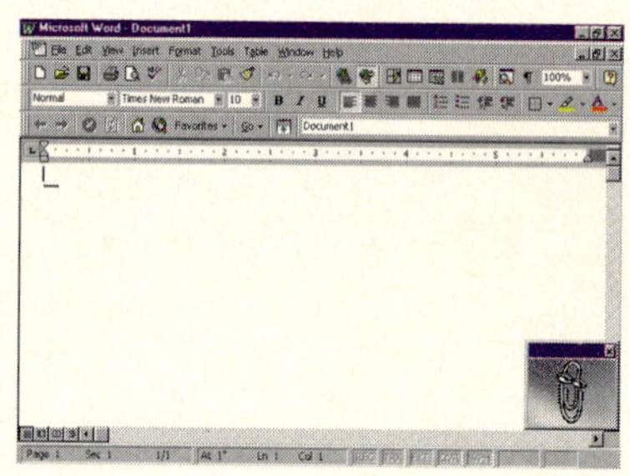

Figure 1.34
The Word application window.

4. **Verify the number of documents that you have opened.**

Window	Click to display the Window menu (Figure 1.38). You should see the names of the two files you have just loaded as well as the name of the blank document (Document2).
4Ch1 Introduction to Databases	Click this document name. You should now see this document displayed in the Word window.

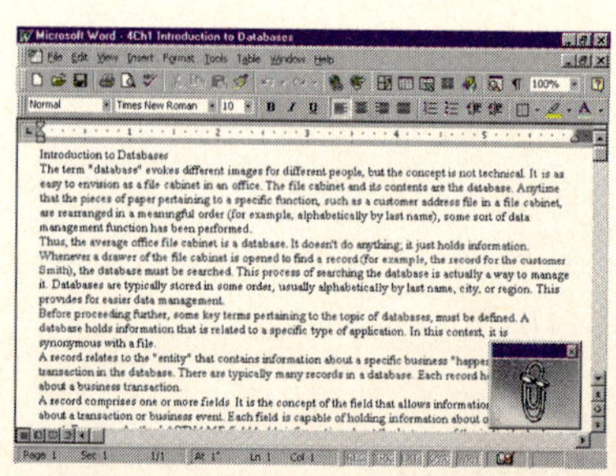

Figure 1.35
The Word window with the 4Ch1 Introduction to Databases document loaded.

3–22 WINDOWS 95

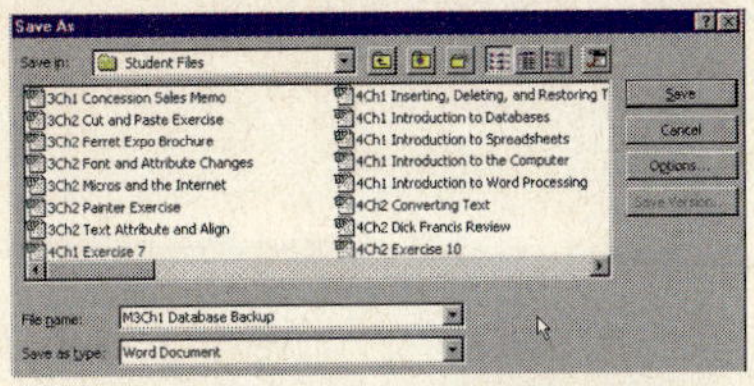

9. **Exit the application.**

Click the Close button at the right end of the title bar. You should return to the Windows desktop.

Figure 1.41
The completed Save As dialog box used to save a copy of the 4Ch1 Introduction to Database document under the name M3Ch1 Database Backup.

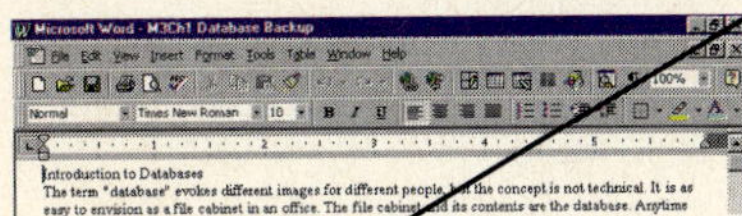

Figure 1.42
The newly specified document name appears in the title bar.

Reinforcing the Exercise

1. You can close a document either by using the File, Close command sequence or by clicking the document's Close button.
2. If you issue a Close command for an unnamed document, the Save As dialog box appears when you indicate that that document is to be saved.
3. You can use the Save As command to create a copy of a document using another name.
4. You can use the New Document button on an application's toolbar to open a blank document.
5. You can use the Windows menu to switch from one open document to another.

PRINTING A DOCUMENT **File, Print, or**

Most Office applications provide two methods for printing a document: issuing the File, Print command sequence or clicking the Print button.

Reinforcing the Exercise sections help students recall and refer to the work they have completed.

Introduction to Windows 95 1–19

want to do anything with that particular menu, you can open an adjacent menu using the right or left arrow key or by clicking with the mouse. If you want to close a menu, position the pointer anywhere outside that menu and click, or press ESC one or more times.

Status Bar

The **status bar** at the bottom of the window provides information on the item you select. The status bar does not appear on every window. If you select an object, for example, you may see information on the number of objects selected and the amount of free space on the disk.

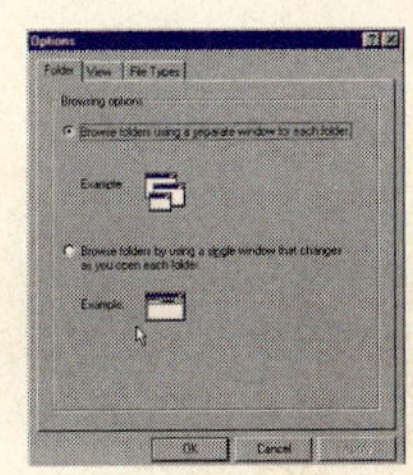

Figure 1.29
The Options dialog box.

Hands-On Exercise: Using Menus

The My Computer window should be visible on the desktop. If it isn't, double-click it to open the window.

1. **Use the mouse to open menus.**

View Click this menu bar option to open the View pull-down menu (Figure 1.30).

Table 1.3 Meanings of Symbols and Conventions Used in Windows Menus

Description	Appearance	Meaning
Ellipsis	. . .	A dialog box will appear when you select this command option. The dialog box contains additional options for this command.
Dimmed entry	Dimmed entry	This command option is not available at this time. You have to enter a previous command before this one becomes available.
Checkmark	✓	This command option is in effect. Selecting this command again disables the command and removes the check mark. More than one of this type of option can be activated.
Dot	●	This command option is in effect. Selecting this command again disables the command and removes the large dot. This differs from the check mark in that only one of these options can be activated at a time.
Keys	CTRL + Z	A key combination (such as CTRL + Z) is a shortcut command for this particular option.
Right triangle	▶	An additional menu of options will appear when you select this option command.

Tables of keyboard or **toolbar icons and symbols** provide students with a quick reference to the conventions and uses of Office 97 applications.

WEB SUPPORT

The Web site created for this text is **http://www.awl.com/office97/**. The site provides an interactive experience for students as they complete exercises in the text that send them to the site for information or files. Duffy teaches students how to view and save graphics, how to navigate on the Web, and how to download files; he even offers help on creating their own home pages. Web-based exercises appear at the end of each session in the Internet Exercises section.

ANCILLARIES

The **Instructor's Manual** offers teaching notes to help integrate current technology (such as the text Web site) into a modern course on Office 97, grading tips, and answer keys.

TECHSUITE PROGRAM

Office 97 applications texts are available separately or in a single *Microsoft Office 97 Professional* volume. The Office 97 Professional suite includes Windows 95, Internet Explorer 3.0, Word 97, Access 97, Excel 97, and PowerPoint 97.

Addison-Wesley realizes that you have specific needs for your lab course, so we offer the quick and affordable TechSuite program so that you can choose what you want. Your choice of lab manuals will be sent to your bookstore, combined in a TechSuite, allowing students to purchase all books in one convenient package at a discount.

Your Addison Wesley Longman representative will be happy to work with you and your bookstore manager to outline the ordering process and provide pricing, ISBNs, and delivery information. Or call 1-800-447-2226 or visit our Web site at http://www.awl.com/he/is/.

ACKNOWLEDGMENTS

I am amazed that ten years have passed since I started the first edition of *Four Software Tools*. At that time, I was totally unaware of the time-consuming efforts needed to produce a college-level textbook. Since then, however, I have developed a sincere appreciation of what is required to make a successful text. The success formula includes family, friends, colleagues, and many individuals in the publishing business. I remain deeply indebted to my wife, Wendy, who encouraged me to write the original version of *Four Software Tools*. Without her encouragement, the original text would never have been finished, and without her continued support, these projects would be impossible to accomplish.

I also want to express my sincere appreciation to the reviewers of this manuscript:

Jill Betts, Tyler Junior College
Bill Daley, University of Oregon
Kathryn A. Drexel, Drexel Associates

Peter Drexel, Plymouth State College
Seth Hock, Columbus State Community College
Marie McCooey, Bryant College
Vincent J. Motto, Asnuntuck Community-Technical College
Stephen C. Solosky, Nassau Community College
Melinda C. White, Santa Fe Community College

Individuals at the publishing company also play an important role. Addison Wesley Longman's editorial staff is superb. With warm feelings, I would like to acknowledge Maureen Allaire, Carol Crowell, and Ed Moura. Maureen initially signed this book and over the years has had much to do with many of my books. I am pleased to be working again with Carol Crowell, who brings a wealth of editorial experience in microcomputer texts. Ed Moura, Editor-in-Chief, brought a number of excellent ideas to this project. Kerry Connor, editorial assistant, made certain that everything was going on an even keel. Bess Deck, Juliet Silveri, Sue Purdy Pelosi and Barbara Conway made the publishing process smooth and professional.

An often overlooked ingredient in the success of textbooks is the publisher's marketing and sales staff. Michelle Hudson's experienced efforts in developing a marketing plan are greatly appreciated. I am convinced that the Addison Wesley Longman sales staff is one of the best in the business.

A dedication is not complete without including my son, Michael. Michael continues to make any writing project a challenge. His requests to go biking, swimming, or pursue a new interest are much appreciated. Michael especially likes to surf the Web to complete homework assignments and has become a ten-year-old master at ferreting out information from the Web.

CONTENTS

COMMON FEATURES OF OFFICE 97 APPLICATIONS

Common Features of Office 97 Applications

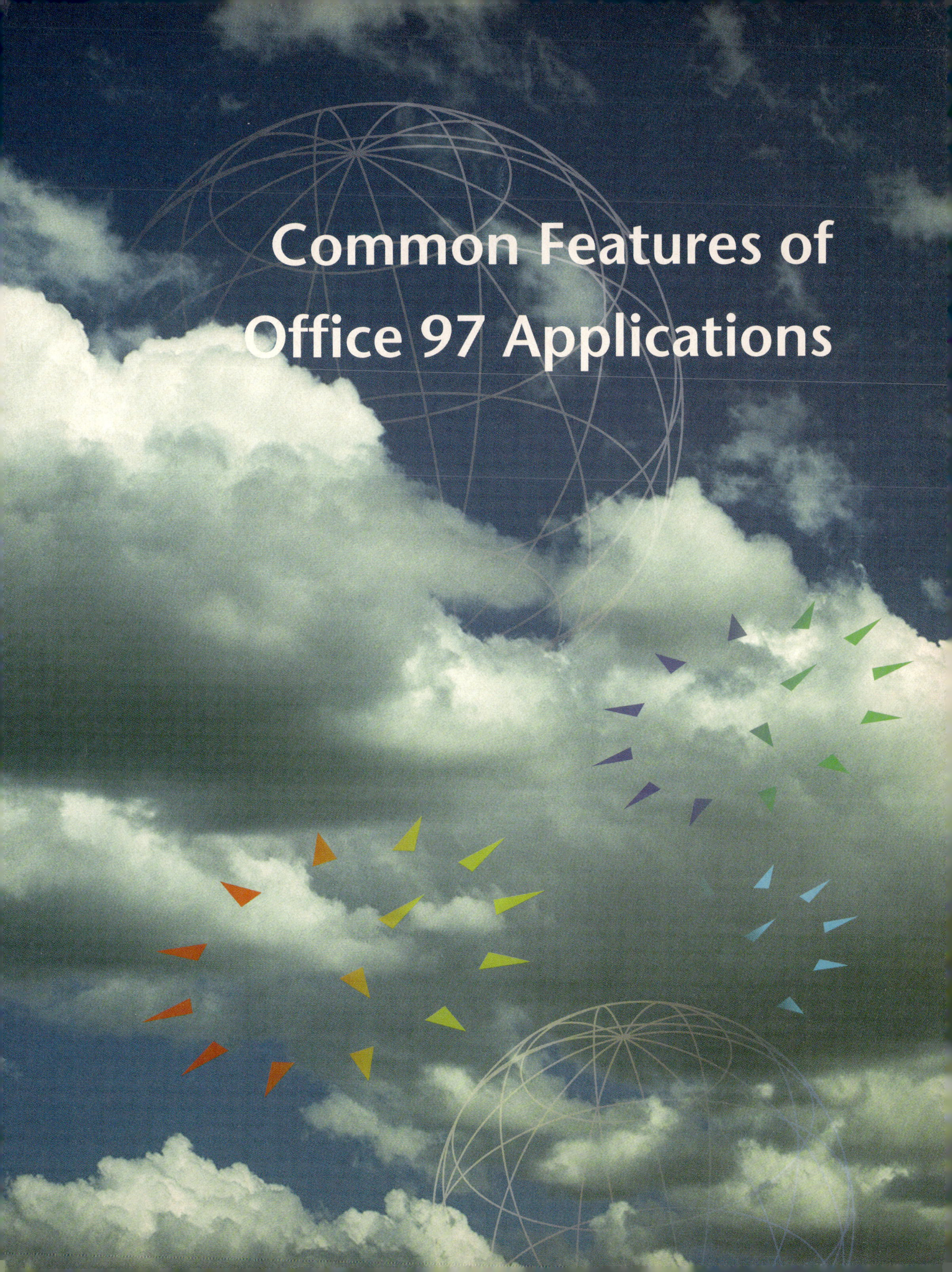

SESSION 1

Using Common Document-Related Commands

After completing this session, you should be able to:

- State the uses of Microsoft Office
- Identify new IntelliMouse commands
- Start an Office application
- Use the Office Assistant
- Indicate when to use each application
- Use the Open and New commands
- Exit an application
- Save a document
- Use the Print and Print Preview commands
- Understand the concept of a binder

Juan and Isabel Ortiz are the managing partners of a sports complex located in a medium-sized town in the Midwest. This complex is owned by a group of investors led by Juan and Isabel. It contains a swimming pool, an exercise facility, a baseball diamond for the local semipro farm team, and a civic arena that seats 6500 people and can be used for the local regional university basketball games as well as special events. Juan and Isabel, along with their investors, are considering building a soccer complex next to their current facility.

In addition to her duties with the sports facility, Isabel also teaches a number of microcomputer-related courses at a local community college and conducts software seminars for local businesses. Since she knows about computers, Isabel also supervises the information processing demands of the sports facility.

Isabel is interested in Microsoft Windows and Office 97 applications because she has been assigned to teach several classes on these programs in the next term. She is also interested in using the application suite in the family business.

Throughout this book, you will be following the Ortizes as they learn about Office 97. As you see how the Ortizes use the software to solve some of their data needs, you will better understand the applicability of using the different parts of Microsoft Office.

INTRODUCTION TO MICROSOFT OFFICE

Microsoft Office is a set of powerful applications, or a **suite,** that have been designed to work together, sharing data so you can combine text, charts, and database information in one document. This book discusses the Professional version of Office, which includes these Microsoft applications: Word, for word processing; Excel, for electronic spreadsheet manipulation; PowerPoint, for making presentation materials; and Access for manipulating databases (Table 1.1). Office also includes a fifth application, such as Outlook, for tracking your schedule. This fifth application varies and will not be covered in this text.

Table 1.1 Components of Office 97

Word	Use this word processing program to manipulate written documents, such as reports, memos, and letters. This software simplifies writing, editing, and printing a document. It can improve your personal productivity by letting you duplicate a document without retyping it and recall a document without leafing through a ton of paper. Word processing does not necessarily reduce the time required to produce a first-draft report from scratch, but it does provide the means to revise and generate an almost perfect document without having to spend hours retyping drafts.
Excel	Use this electronic spreadsheet program to manipulate various data that can be arranged in rows and columns. A cell can contain text, a number, or a formula that has a relationship with other cells. Whenever you change the contents of one cell, the spreadsheet automatically recalculates the values in other cells, allowing you to easily ask "what-if" questions.
Access	Use this database management software to organize, update, and store records and tables in virtually unlimited ways. You can quickly get information from a database by asking a question, or querying, and can create reports concerning a specific type of customer. It saves you vast amounts of time by automating procedures that manually require sifting through mountains of paper.
PowerPoint	Use this presentation software package to create slides or transparencies for a presentation. You can also prepare the lecture notes and audience handouts. This program also offers a variety of graphic images that you can use to make your presentations more interesting and effective.

As mentioned in Session 1 of the Windows module, the Windows operating system standardizes the computer and software environment in which you work. This means that many concepts that you learn for one Windows application (such as how to use the menu system) also apply to other applications. You will also find that features incorporated in one application are used in the same way in all applications in a suite. All Office 97 software applications are **Web aware,** which means that each application can be used to access or generate HTML documents. HTML documents can be stored on your computer or accessed from a specific location on the World Wide Web. For instance, you can use Excel to access information in an HTML document somewhere on the Web and incorporate that information in an open workbook.

Figure 1.1
Shortcut icons for four of the Office applications shown with the Office shortcut bar.

INTELLIMOUSE

With the introduction of Office 97, Microsoft offers a mouse, called **IntelliMouse,** that can perform a wider variety of functions than a regular mouse (Table 1.2). The IntelliMouse looks like a regular mouse except it has a rotating rubber wheel called the wheel button. Using the wheel button is an alternative to using scroll bars or other controls for moving through a document. Before you can use the functions discussed in Table 1.2, the software you use must be programmed to accept these types of mouse commands (all Office 97 applications support the IntelliMouse).

Table 1.2 IntelliMouse Capabilities

Scroll	Turn the wheel button with your finger to scroll up or down.
Pan	Hold the wheel button down, and drag the mouse for continuous scrolling. The farther you move the mouse the faster the panning movement goes.
Zoom	Hold down CTRL as you roll the wheel button to enlarge the screen display.
DataZoom	In outline mode, hold down SHIFT as you roll the wheel button to get into or out of detail in worksheets, Internet pages, or documents.

STARTING AN OFFICE APPLICATION

Microsoft Office provides three ways to start an application:

- Double-click the icon on the desktop that represents the application. This icon is called a **shortcut icon** (Figure 1.1).
- Invoke the Start, Programs command sequence.
- Open an associated file.

Shortcut Icons

Check to see if your screen displays shortcut icons like those shown in Figure 1.1. Such shortcut icons may have been placed on your desktop screen by your school computer lab administrator. You can double-click one of these icons to start the application it represents. Notice that shortcut icons have a curved arrow embedded in a square to indicate that they are indeed shortcuts.

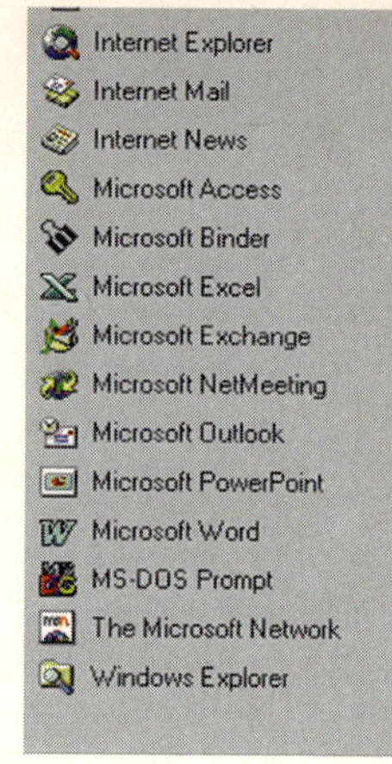

Figure 1.2
A list of Office-related programs displayed in the Programs menu invoked using the Start, Programs command sequence.

Using the Start Button 

The menus invoked by clicking the Start button can also be used to start an Office application program. You first click the Start button to activate the Start menu, and then you point to Programs to activate that menu.

The next action you take depends on what appears on the Programs menu. If single application programs are listed, as shown in Figure 1.2, then you can click the desired program and a window will open for that application. If a Microsoft Office option appears on the Programs menu, click that, and then click the desired application when the menu for Office appears.

✓ *On Your Own*

Your version of Microsoft Office may include a **shortcut bar** (Figure 1.1), which is a long, narrow bar that appears at the top of the screen. The shortcut bar allows you to quickly access existing documents or create new ones. It also provides direct access to the Schedule+ or Outlook feature (not covered in this text), as well as methods for accessing the Help feature or additional information that might be stored on a CD.

If the shortcut bar appears on your screen, experiment with its various buttons. Remember, click the Close button of any dialog box or window that you want to exit.

Using an Associated Document

As discussed in Session 2 of the Windows module, you can start an application by double-clicking the icon for an associated document. You can see associated documents when you are viewing the contents of a disk or folder using the My Computer window (Figure 1.3). If the icon for the associated document has an *X*, Excel starts and the document is loaded. If the icon has a *W*, Microsoft Word starts and the document is loaded. (Review Session 2 of the Windows module if you have any questions about other associated document icons.)

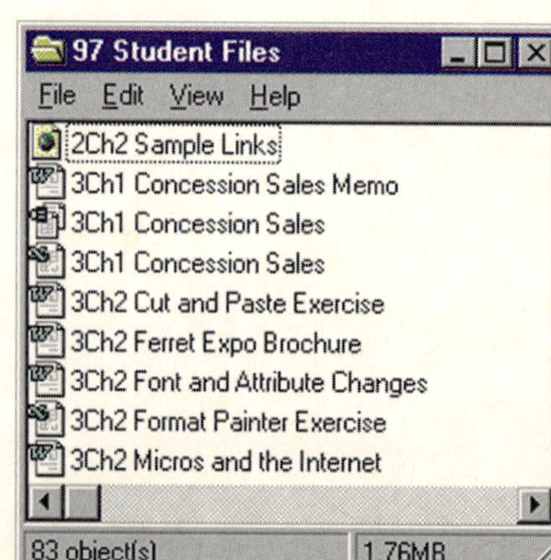

Figure 1.3
The 97 Student Files folder window with files shown for the Internet Explorer, Word, Excel, and the Binder.

USING THE OFFICE ASSISTANT

Every Office application provides help through a feature called the **Office Assistant.** There are several types of Office Assistants available. All appear as a box in the lower-right corner of the screen, and the graphic included in that box varies depending on the type of Office Assistant you choose. Figure 1.4 shows the default Office Assistant called Clippit.

Usually, the Office Assistant feature is activated when you start any Office Application. If it does not appear on your screen, you can activate it by clicking the Office Assistant button on the toolbar. Initially the Office Assistant appears something like Clippit shown in Figure 1.4. The appearance of the box changes, however, as you perform tasks within that application.

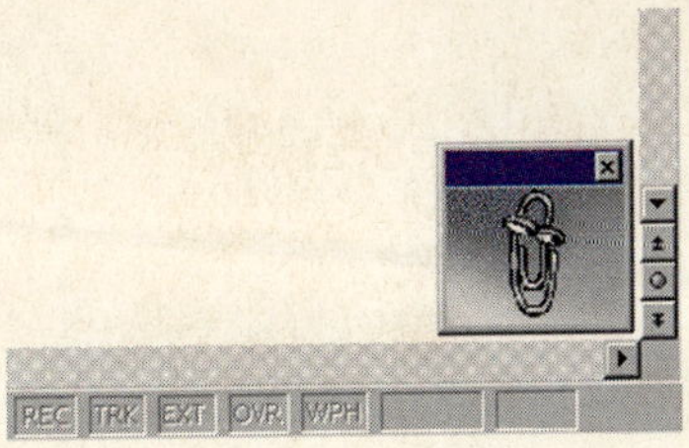

Figure 1.4
Clippit, the default Office Assistant.

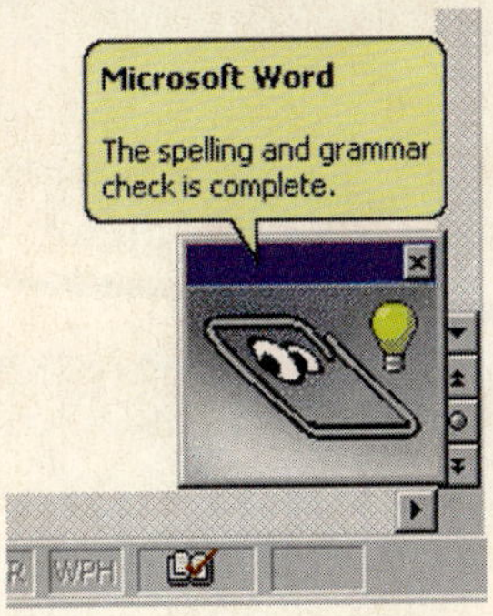

Figure 1.5
The Office Assistant offering to help you with the task of checking spelling.

If you perform a task that the Office Assistant thinks can be done more efficiently, it offers help without waiting for you to ask. A light bulb appears in the upper-right corner of the Office Assistant box (Figure 1.5). The appearance of the graphic changes, and a bubble displays a brief statement about the task you just performed. When you click an Office Assistant box with this appearance, the Office Assistant provides additional information on how you can make the task easier (Figure 1.6).

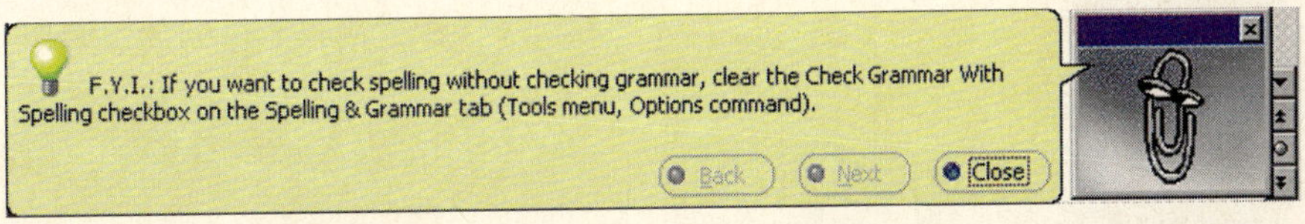

Figure 1.6
Additional information provided by the Office Assistant on using Word's spelling checker efficiently.

If you run into a problem and want the Office Assistant to help you, you can click the Office Assistant box to get its attention. The Office Assistant should look like that shown in Figure 1.7. If, for example, you want information about printing, you type the word *printing* in the box and then click the Search button. A list of topics appears, as shown in Figure 1.8. You can click on any topic to receive further information.

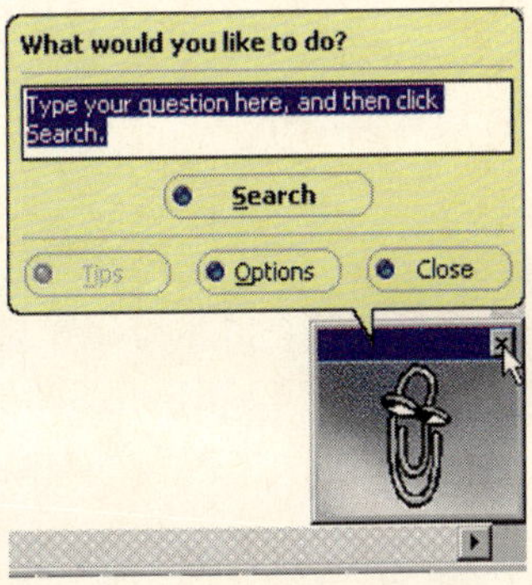

Figure 1.7
The Office Assistant ready to help you.

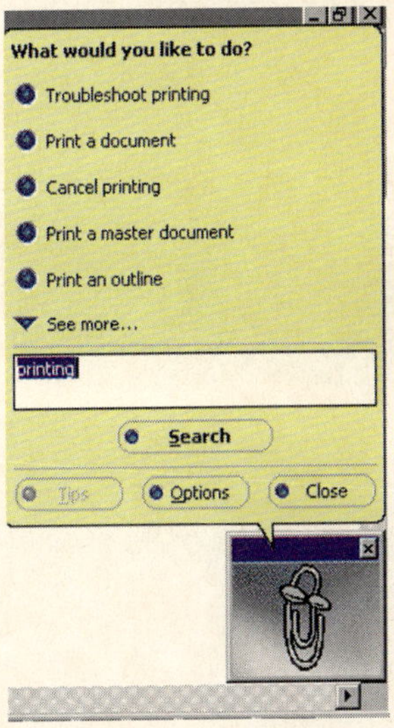

Figure 1.8
A list of topics related to printing.

Information about the Print a document option appears in Figure 1.9. As you can see, this option generates a list of print-

TIMELY TIP

If you have a sound system hooked to your computer, you can hear the Office Assistant making various sounds as you enter an Office document or perform tasks on a document.

ing-related topics. Choosing the Print a range of pages option results in the Help screen shown in Figure 1.10.

You can change the type of Office Assistant from the default of Clippit to one of about eight other versions Office provides. When you right-click on the Office Assistant box, a context menu appears. Click the Options menu item to open the Office Assistant dialog box. Click the Gallery tab, and your screen should appear similar to the one shown in Figure 1.11 and Figure 1.12. Follow the instructions given in the dialog box to examine the various Office Assistants and make your selection.

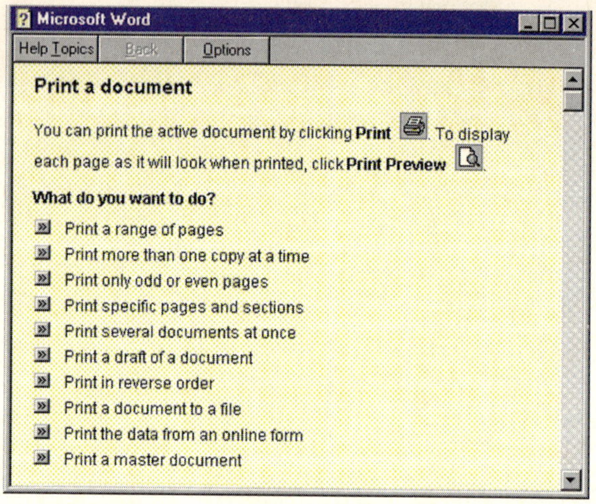

Figure 1.9
The Office Assistant generated this list of printing-related topics.

USING THE OPEN DIALOG BOX

File, Open, or

You access the Open dialog box by clicking the Open button on any Office application toolbar or by invoking the File, Open Command Sequence. The Open dialog box loads a document so you can work with it. No matter how you access it, the Open Dialog box always looks like Figure 1.13. It provides a number of features that make accessing and displaying document names easier. It also allows you to perform searches as well as execute basic file maintenance tasks.

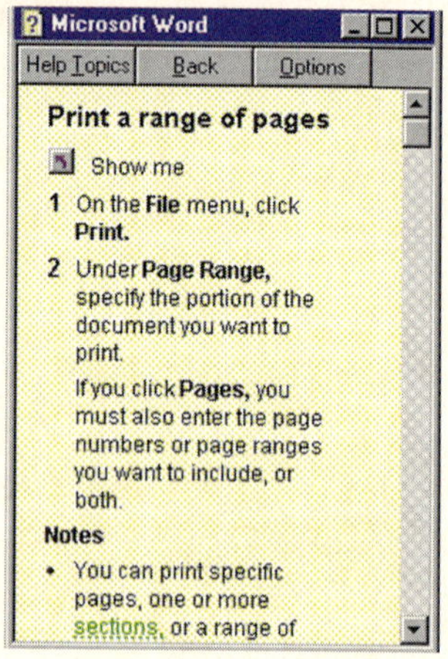

Figure 1.10
The Office Assistant's information on printing a range of pages.

Changing Folders for Document Retrieval

By default, the folder called My Documents found on drive C appears in the Look in list box. This folder was created automatically when Microsoft Office was installed. Unless you tell Office differently, all documents are automatically saved and loaded from this folder. To select a different folder, click

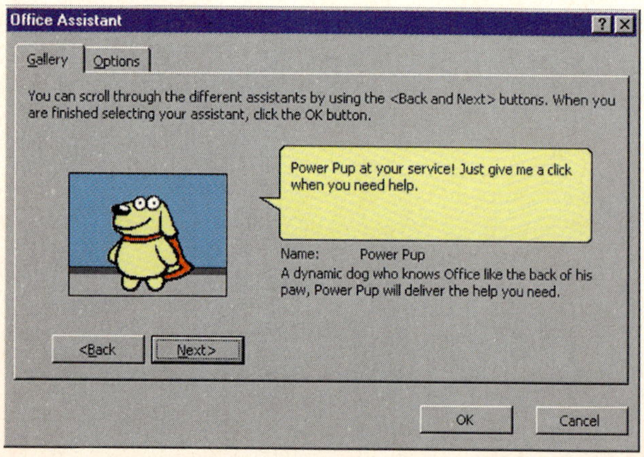

Figure 1.11
The Office Assistant dialog box allows you to choose different assistants, such as Power Pup.

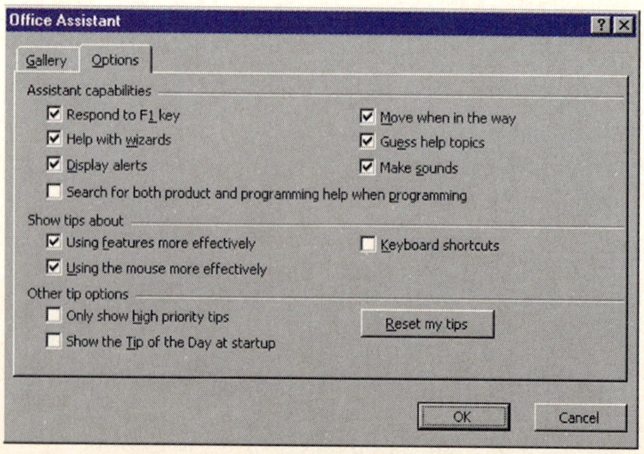

Figure 1.12
The Options tab of the Office Assistant dialog box.

the down arrow at the right end of the list box. A hierarchical list of drives and folders appears (Figure 1.14). You first select a different drive, if necessary, and then double-click the folder you want to use for loading and saving documents.

Figure 1.15 shows that a folder called Student Files is selected, and the documents in that folder are displayed in the Open dialog box.

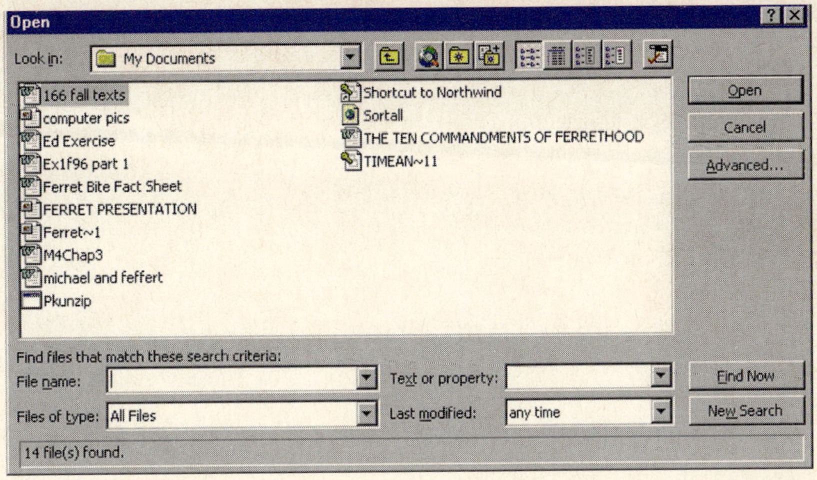

Figure 1.13
The standard Open dialog box for any Office application. The file type varies among applications.

Controlling Document Display

Microsoft Office provides considerable flexibility in how folder and document information in the Open dialog box is displayed. You control the display by using the buttons across the top of the dialog box. These buttons are summarized in Table 1.3.

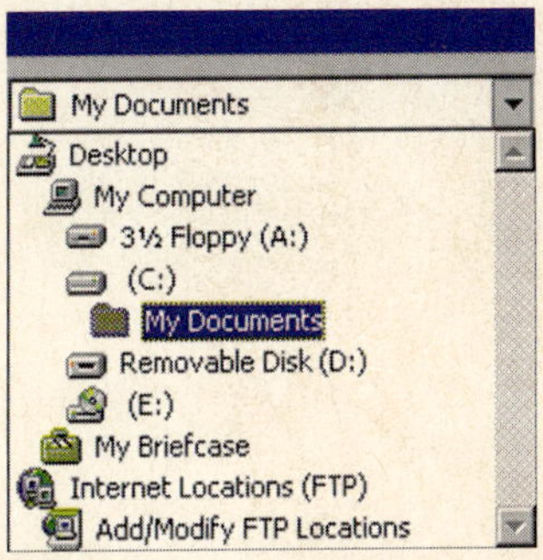

Figure 1.14
The Look in selection box for changing the disk or folder used to load and save documents.

Performing a Search

The Open dialog box also allows you to search documents and folders. The search can be based on document names or document contents. You can also perform more exotic searches by first clicking the Advanced button and then using the Advanced dialog box.

Performing File Maintenance

Once you have one or more documents selected in the Open dialog box, you can perform a number of tasks on them by clicking the right mouse button to open the context menu shown in Figure 1.16. For instance, you

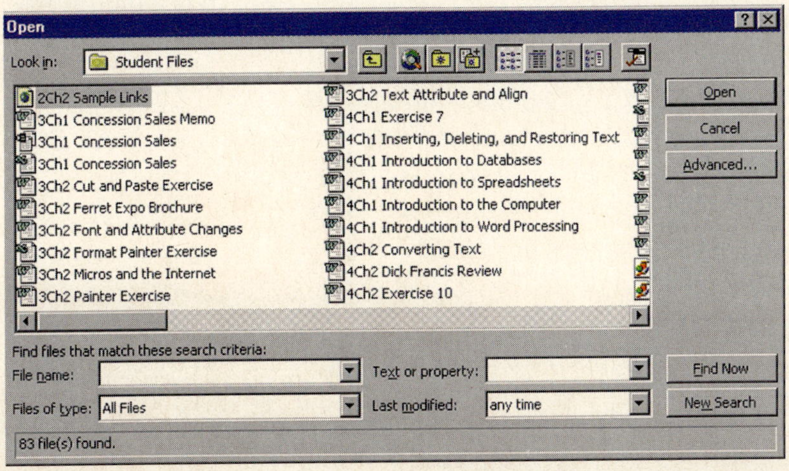

Figure 1.15
The documents found in the Student Files folder displayed in the Open dialog box.

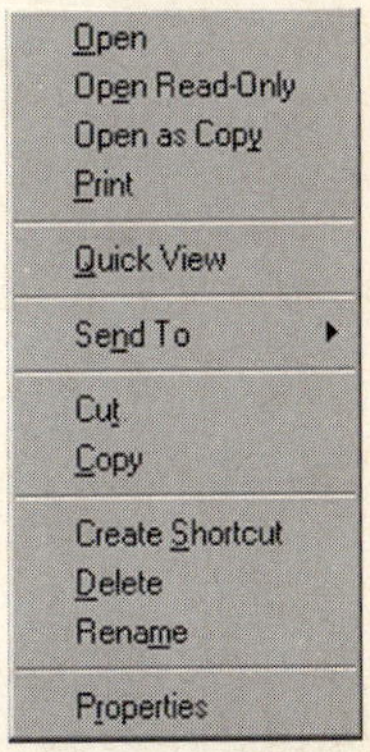

Figure 1.16
The Open dialog box context menu, where you can perform many of the same file maintenance tasks that you perform in a folder window.

Table 1.3 Buttons in the Open Dialog Box

Button	Name of Button	Function
	Up One Level	Moves you up to the next folder in this hierarchy
	Search the Web	Opens the Search page for your Internet browser
	Look in Favorites	Allows you easily to locate frequently used documents
	Add to Favorites	Adds any selected objects to the Favorites folder, where they can be accessed by clicking the Look in Favorites button
	List	Shows the names of the files, each with a large icon
	Details	Lists each object on a separate line along with the object size, type of file, and date the object was last modified
	Properties	Provides additional information on a document such as the title, subject, and author
	Preview	Splits the dialog box and lets you preview the selected Office document before you access it from an application
	Commands and Settings	Opens a pull-down menu that allows you to print, sort, or perform a search of folders

can delete, rename, print, or preview documents by using the Open dialog box context menu. These tasks are similar to ones you do on the Windows desktop or in a folder window.

Hands-On Exercise: Opening an Existing Document

Isabel decides that she wants to examine some of the Office features that she can use to open documents. In this exercise you first examine how you can move around the disk using the Look in list box, then examine the Word document 4Ch1 Introduction to Databases. It also acquaints you with several features of the

On Your Own

When many different people are using software in a computer lab, the Office Assistant does not offer the same assistance. To reset the Office Assistant feature, or to invoke a different Office Assistant, you must open the Office Assistant dialog box by doing the following:

1. If necessary, activate the Office Assistant.
2. Position the pointer on the Office Assistant and right-click. A context menu opens.
3. Click Options to open the Office Assistant dialog box (Figure 1.12).
4. Click the Reset my tips button. You will now see the Office Assistant box every time you work in Office.
5. The Gallery tab allows you to select a new Office Assistant.
6. Click the OK button to close the Office Assistant dialog box.

Open dialog box. You should be at the Windows desktop and should not have any applications open.

1. **Open the document.**

Click the Start button to open the Start menu.

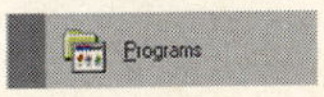

Click to display the Programs menu. If necessary, click the Office 97 entry.

Click to start Word.

Open the Open dialog box by clicking this button below the menu bar. Your screen should now look like Figure 1.17. You should see any documents that occupy the My Documents folder on the disk (yours will look differently than Figure 1.17). This is the default folder displayed by Microsoft Office whenever an Open command is issued.

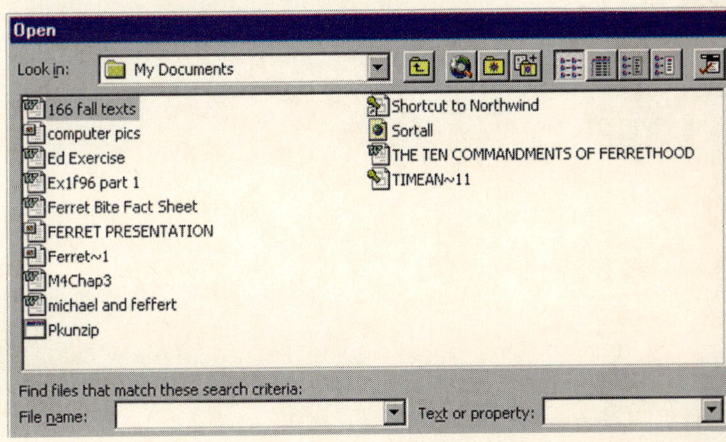

Figure 1.17
The Open dialog box with the documents that reside in the My Documents folder (the Office default storage area). Yours will look different.

Click this entry of the Look in list box to display a list of available storage resources (Figure 1.18).

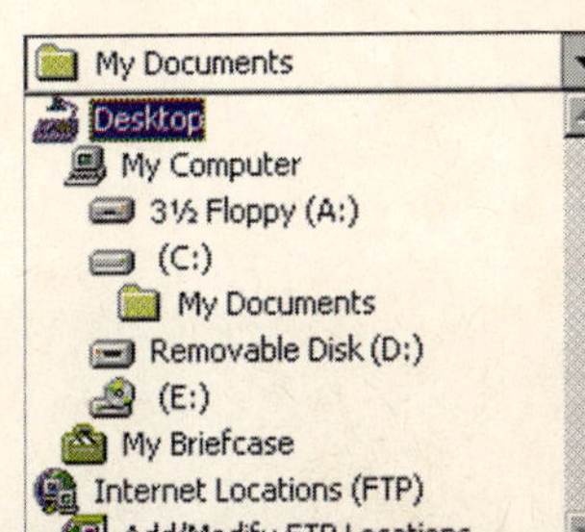

Figure 1.18
The available storage resources on the computer are displayed in the Look in list box.

2. **If necessary, activate the area containing your student files.** This example assumes that those student files reside on drive A. If your files reside on a network drive or in a directory on a fixed disk, your instructor will provide you with the proper command sequence. Be sure to write down that command sequence so you can use it in the future.

Click the drive A option to display a list of documents that reside on that drive (Figure 1.19). If the Open dialog box does not list the documents as shown in Figure 1.19, click the List button.

3. **Activate an application by double-clicking an associated document.**

4Ch1 Introduction to Databases Double-click this file name. Microsoft Word loads the document. You should now see a screen like that shown in Figure 1.20.

4. **Close the document and open the Open dialog box.**

File Click to open the File menu.

Close Click to clear the document screen. If a dialog box appears asking whether you want to save the document, click the No button.

Open the Open dialog box.

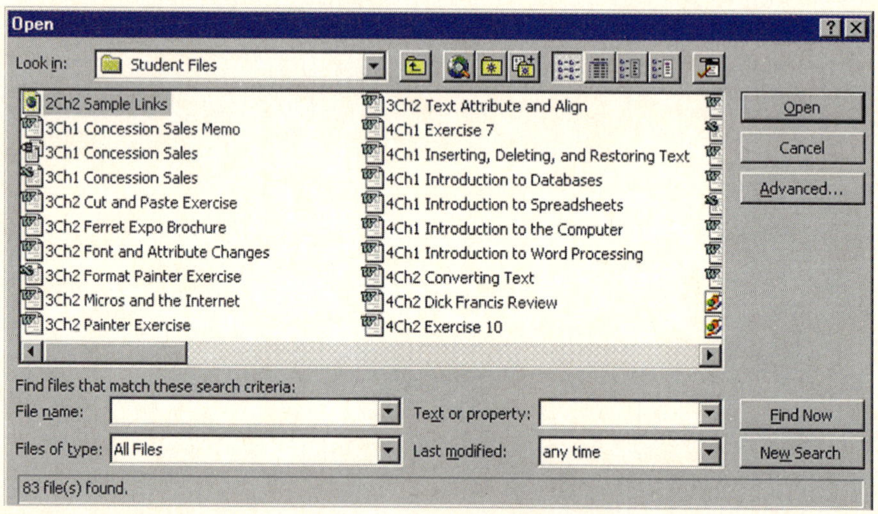

Figure 1.19
The documents that accompany the textbook (your display may be different).

5. Use the command buttons.

3Ch1 Concession Sales Memo Click to select this Word document.

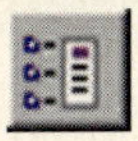

Click the Preview button. The document list box now divides in half. The left half lists the documents, and the right half displays the contents of the selected Word document (Figure 1.21).

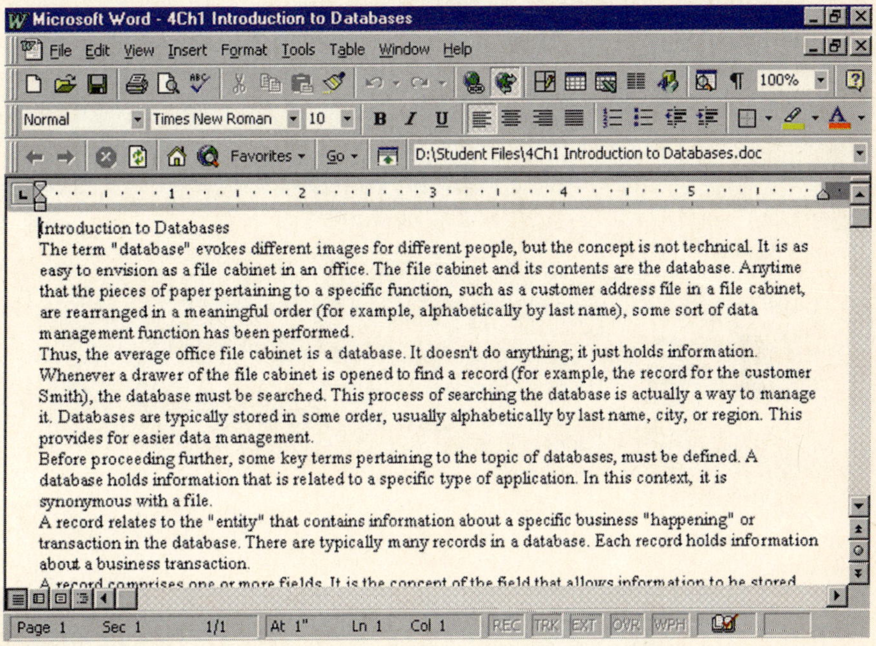

Figure 1.20
The 4Ch1 Introduction to Databases document loaded into Word.

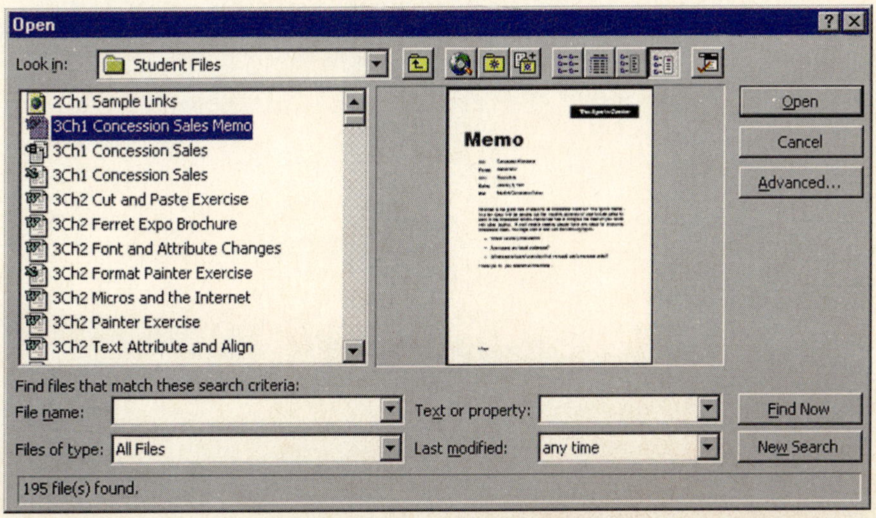

Figure 1.21
The 3Ch1 Concession Sales Memo document previewed in the Open dialog box.

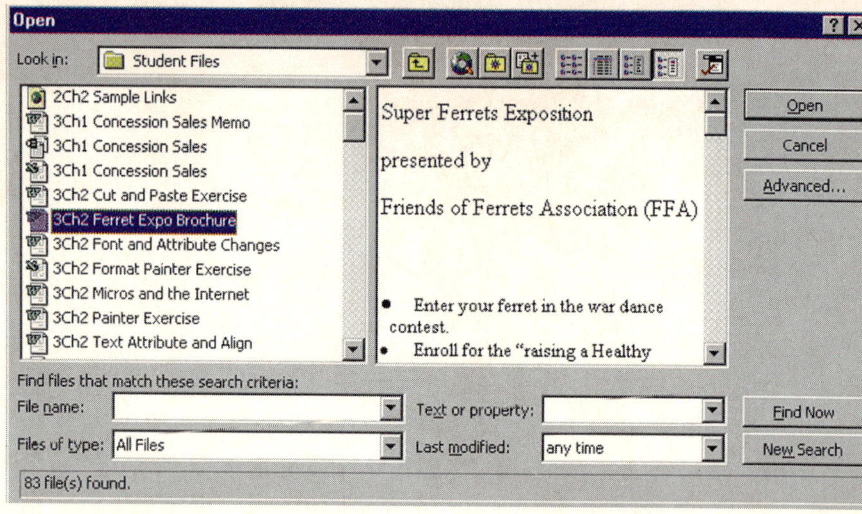

Figure 1.22
The previewed 3Ch2 Ferret Expo Brochure Word document.

3Ch2 Ferret Expo Brochure Click to select this Word document. The contents should now appear in the preview box (Figure 1.22).

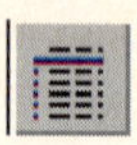
Click to display multiple columns of information for the displayed documents (Figure 1.23).

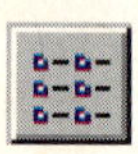
Click to return the document display to icons and names.

3Ch1 Concession Sales Click to select this Excel workbook file.

Click to display the summary data for the document, including the author's name, date of last modification, and so forth (Figure 1.24).

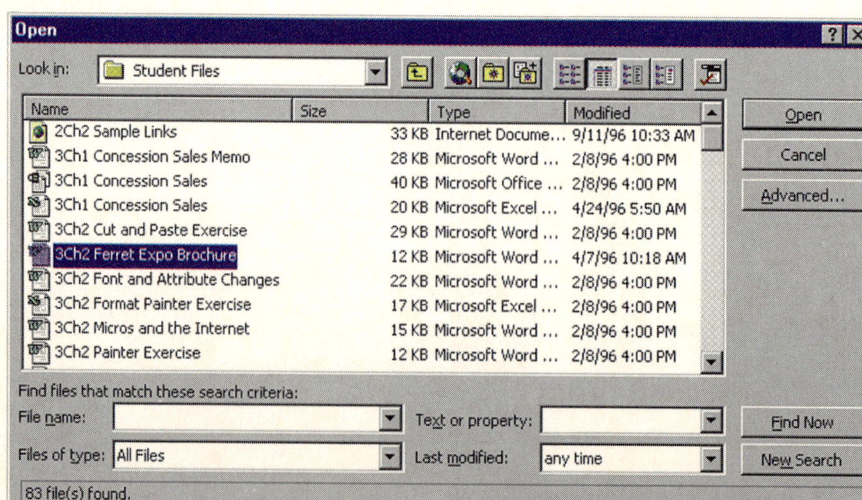

Figure 1.23
The Open dialog box with the Details button invoked.

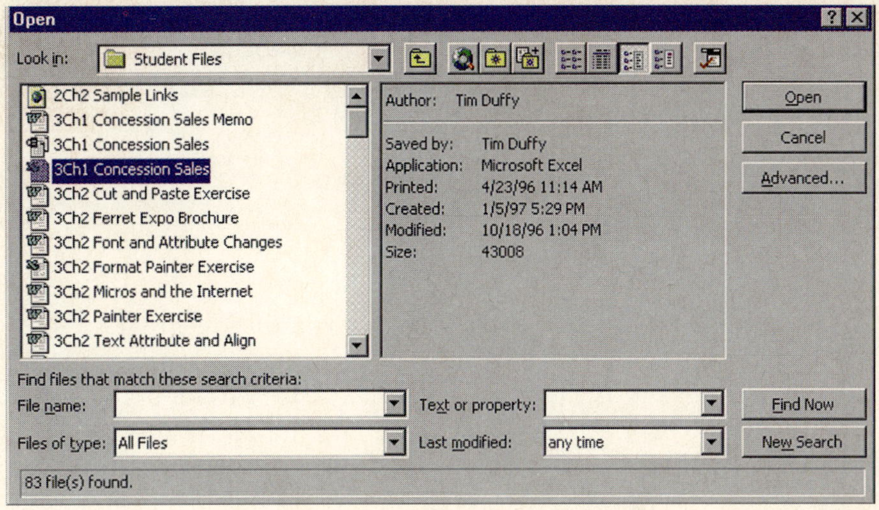

Figure 1.24
The 3Ch1 Concession Sales Excel workbook shown with the Properties box invoked.

6. **List all documents that contain the term *word processing.***

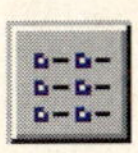

Click to display document names.

Text or property: Click this box to enter the text to be located.

Type: **word processing** The Open dialog box should now look like Figure 1.25.

Click to display a list of the documents that contain the desired text, *word processing* (Figure 1.26).

Click to return to the document window.

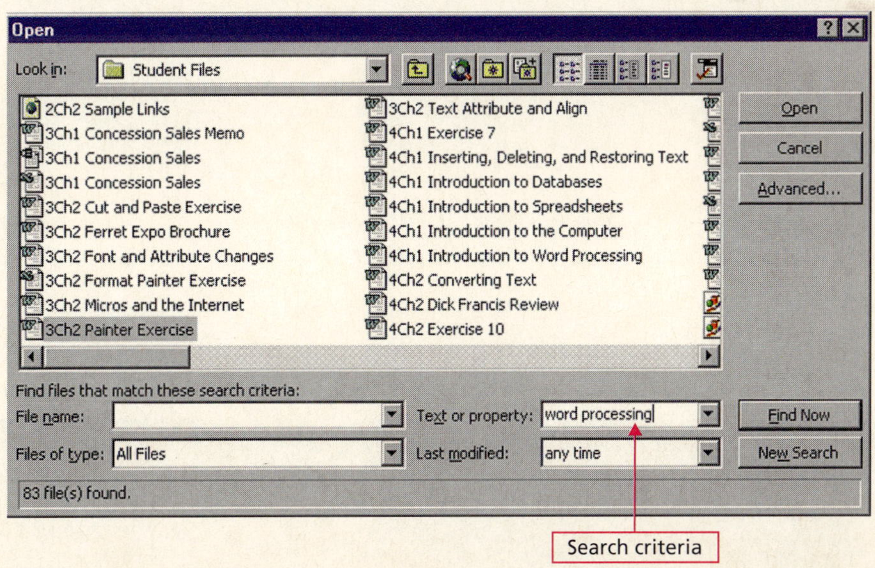

Figure 1.25
The Open dialog box with the search criteria *word processing.*

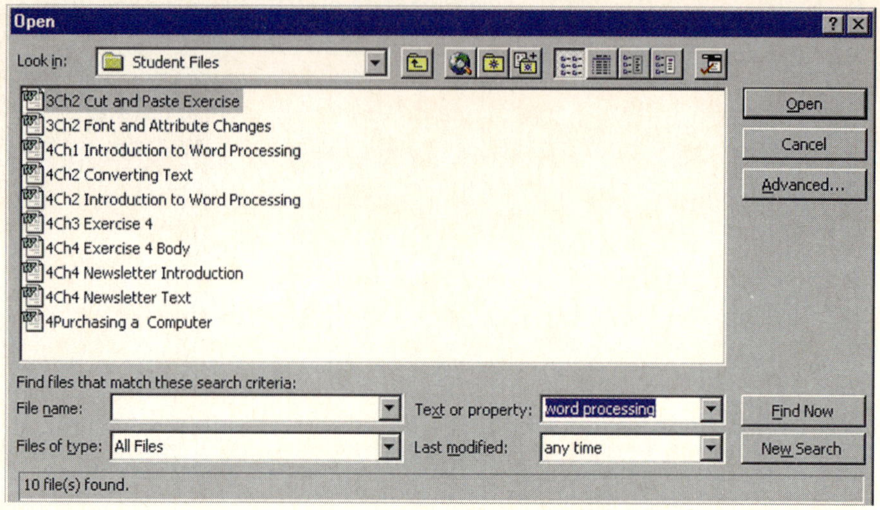

Figure 1.26
The list of files that contain the text *word processing*.

7. **Exit the application and return to the desktop.**

Click the Close button of the Word title bar to return to the Windows desktop. If you are prompted about saving the file, click the No button.

Reinforcing the Exercise

1. You use the Look in list box to examine files that reside on various computer drives and resources.
2. The Up One Level button allows you to move up one level in a folder hierarchy.
3. The Preview button allows you to examine the contents of an Office document.
4. You can perform a search using the Open dialog box.
5. The Properties button allows you to see the name of the designated author of a document.

CLOSING A DOCUMENT

File, Close or 

Once you have opened a document and made changes to it, you must close it before you can close the application. In addition, you may want to close a document before you move to another document or application. You can close any Office application document by clicking on that document's Close button. The Close button for a maximized document window is always located at the right end of the menu bar. If you have not saved the document before, a dialog box like that shown in Figure 1.27 appears, prompting you about saving the file. Click the Yes button to save changes to the document and clear the document window. Click the No button to clear the screen

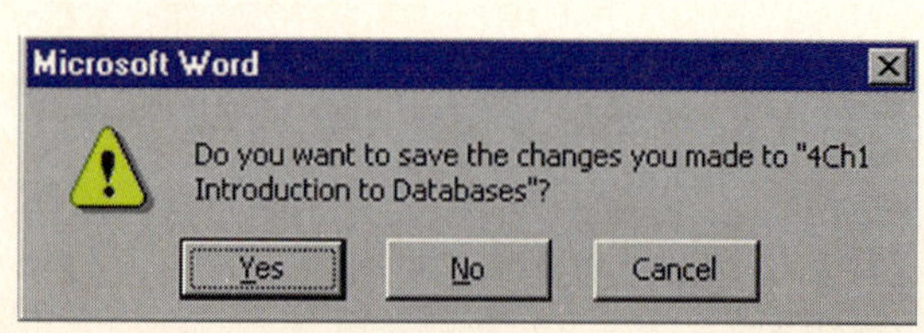

Figure 1.27
The dialog box for saving a document that appears after you have issued the Close command.

without saving the document. Click the Cancel button to return to the document.

If the Office Assistant is present when you close a document, your screen will appear with the Assistant depicted in Figure 1.28.

If you are working with an unnamed document that you've never saved before and decide to close it, a Save As dialog box appears, prompting you for a filename. The Save As dialog box is discussed in detail later in this session.

After you close a document, you can open another document or start a new application.

EXITING AN APPLICATION

File, Exit, or

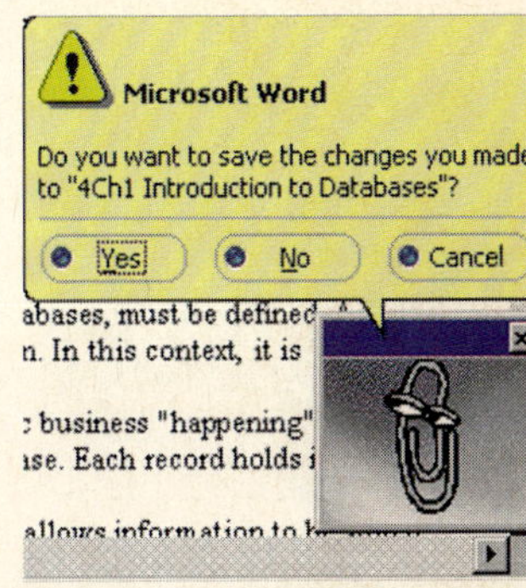

Figure 1.28
The Office Assistant querying about saving a changed file.

Once you decide to exit an application program, you have several alternatives. You can issue a File, Exit command sequence or click the Close button on that application's title bar. Make certain that you click the Close button on the title bar and not the Close button on the menu bar or the document title bar (that will only close the open document).

If you have not previously saved the document, a dialog box like that shown in Figure 1.27 or Figure 1.28 appears, prompting you about saving the file. If you are working with an unnamed document and decide to save it, a Save As dialog box appears prompting you for the new filename. The Save As dialog box is discussed in detail later in this session.

OPENING A NEW DOCUMENT

You may want to start a new document instead of working on an existing document. Again, each Office application provides a button on a toolbar that allows you to accomplish this task easily.

When you click the New button on the Word application's toolbar, the window shown in Figure 1.29 appears. The window consists of a blank document with the default name Document followed by a number.

To move between documents that have been opened in different windows in an application, open the Window menu from the menu bar. At the bottom of the Window pull-down menu is a list of all documents that are open for that application (Figure 1.30). Notice that what looks like a depressed button with a check mark appears next to the active document (the one currently displayed on-screen). Click any other document listed on this menu to make it the active document.

SAVING A DOCUMENT

File, Save As, or 

You have already been introduced to one method of saving a file: by issuing the Close command. You can also use the File or Save As command.

Save As Command

Invoking the Save As command opens the Save As dialog box (Figure 1.31). This dialog box opens automatically whenever you save a document for the first time. You can also open it anytime you want to save the active document in a different folder or change the name of the document. Notice that, for a new document, Word provides a default name, Document, followed by a number. For example, the figure shows the name Document2.

Notice that many of the buttons that appear in the Save As dialog box also appear in the Open dialog box. Refer to the discussion of the Open dialog box if you have any questions about the purpose of these buttons.

The File name list box at the bottom of the screen displays either the original filename or the default filename (for a new document). If you want to change that name, simply start typing, and the existing characters are replaced by the new characters. To display a list of filenames that you have accessed in the past, click the down arrow at the right end of the list box. Double-click the desired filename to place it in the list box and close the list.

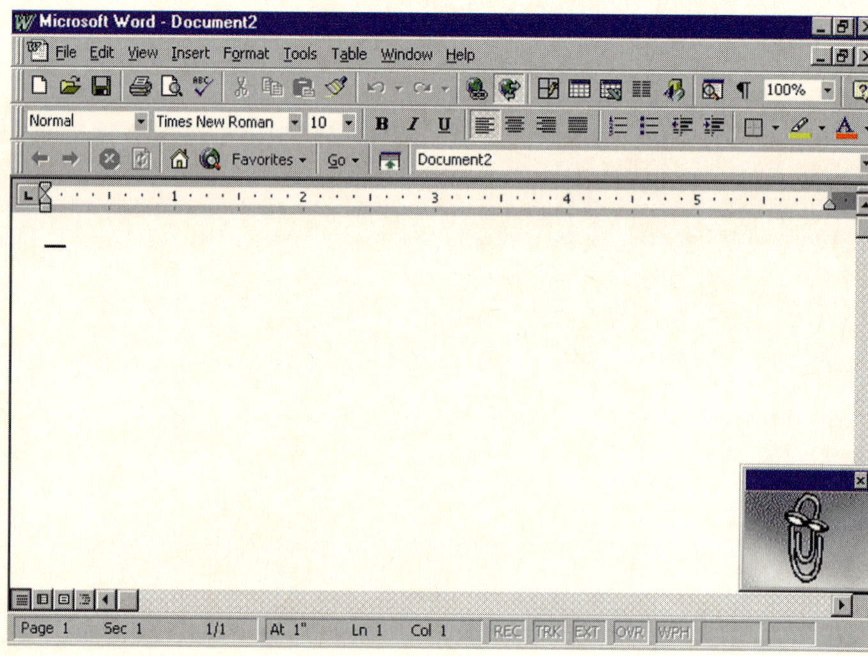

Figure 1.29
A new document, with the default name *Document2,* opened using the New button.

The Save as type list box controls the format used to save the document. If you want to save the file in a format that can be used by another application, click the down arrow to see a list of available formats (Figure 1.32) and then click the desired format.

Once you have entered the new filename (along with any other needed changes), click the Save button to execute the command and return to the document. If you click the Cancel or Exit command, you will return to the desktop without changing the filename.

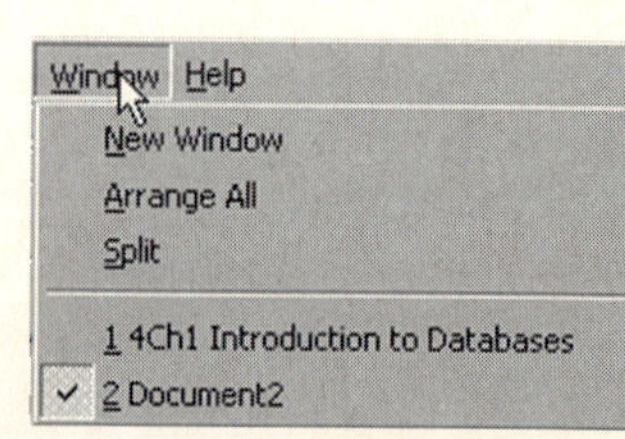

Figure 1.30
The Window menu, which lists all open documents allows you to switch between documents easily.

Save Command File, Save or

The Save command allows you to immediately save the active document. You may use the Save command periodically to save any changes that you have made in a document. You are generally encouraged to use some version of the Save command every 10 to 15 minutes or so to save your work to disk. Then, if the power goes out, all that you will have to redo is the work you've done since the last Save command.

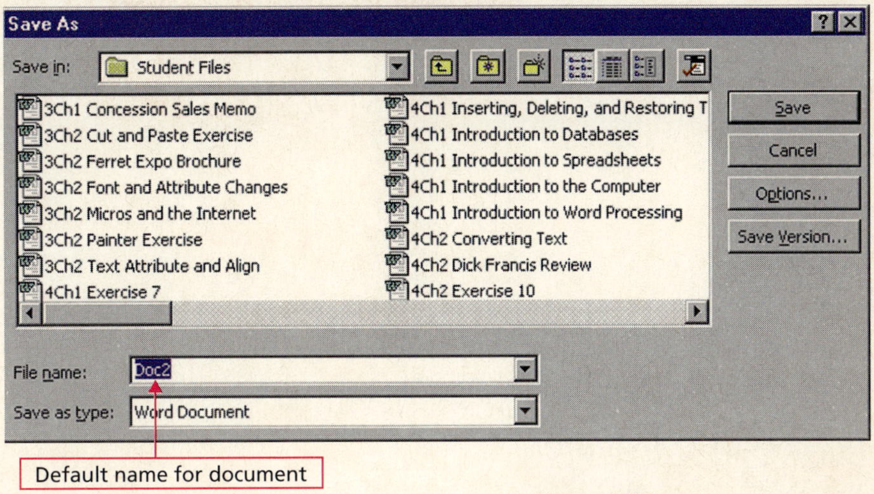

Figure 1.31
Using the Save As dialog box, you can save a document for the first time, change the name of a document, or store a document in a different location on the disk.

Providing Web Access to a File

Office applications permit you to save just about any document as an HTML file using the command sequence File, Save as HTML. It invokes the Save As HTML dialog box shown in Figure 1.33.

This feature allows you to create a document that you can retrieve directly using Internet Explorer. You can save a file as an HTML document on your local disk, or you can specify a URL to which you want the document saved.

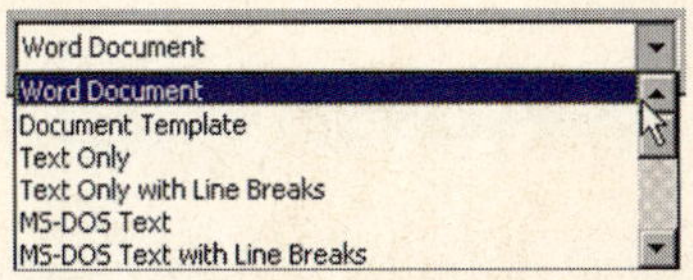

Figure 1.32
The available formats that Word can use to save a file to disk.

TIMELY TIP

Office has a built-in automatic save feature that you can use to restore some of your lost work. This AutoSave feature saves every 10 minutes or so. If you restart your computer after a power outage and then start the software application that you were using when you lost power, you will be stepped through the procedure of recovering the data. However you can recover only the data entered prior to the last AutoSave operation.

This feature can be activated by issuing the Tool, Options command sequence. When the Options dialog box opens, click the Save tab and examine the AutoRecover portion of the tab.

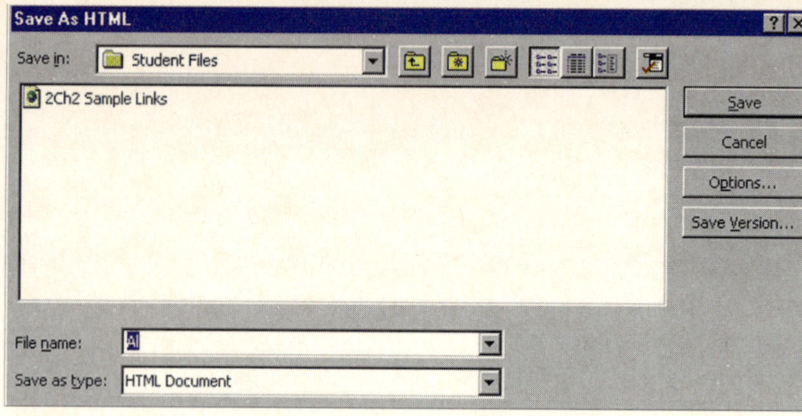

Figure 1.33
The Save As HTML dialog box allows you to create a file that can be accessed using a Web Browser like Internet Explorer.

Hands-On Exercise: Using File Commands

Isabel wants to examine several of the file-oriented commands that are found in various Office applications.

1. **Start Word.**

Click to open the Start menu.

Click to open the Programs menu. If your computer has an Office 97 option, click that option.

Click to start Word. You should see a screen like that shown in Figure 1.34.

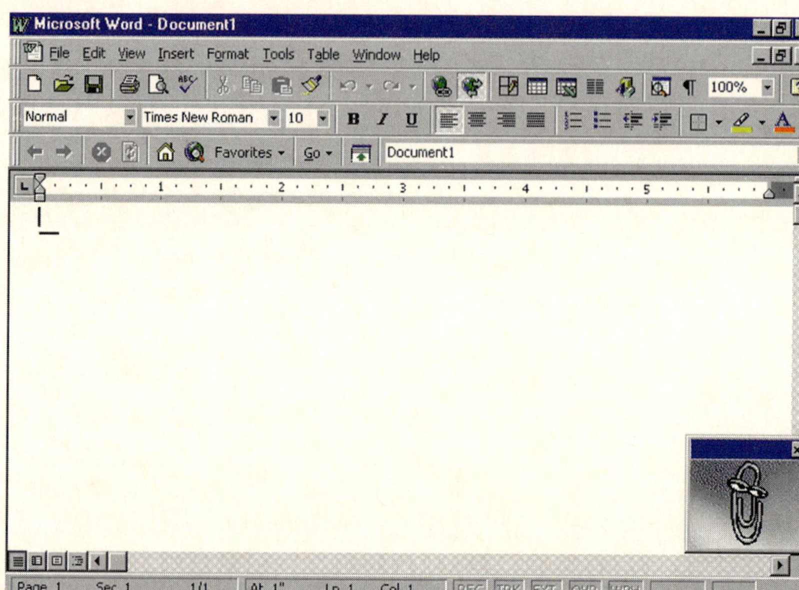

Figure 1.34
The Word application window.

2. **Open two documents using the Open button on the toolbar.**

Click to open the Open dialog box. Make the necessary changes to access the disk or folder containing the student files used with this textbook.

4Ch1 Introduction to Databases Double-click this name to load the document (you may have to use the scroll bar to display this filename). Your screen should now look like Figure 1.35.

Click to open the Open dialog box again.

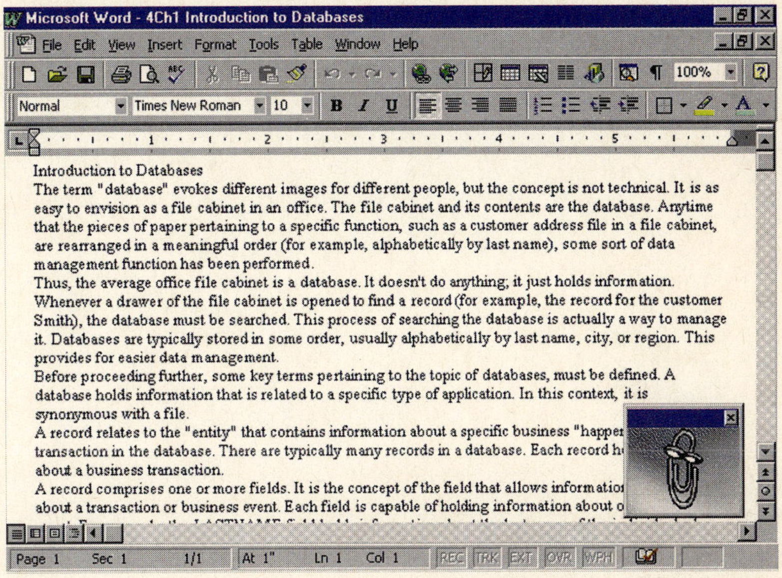

Figure 1.35
The Word window with the 4Ch1 Introduction to Databases document loaded.

4Ch1 Introduction to Spreadsheets Double-click this name to load the document. Your screen should now look like Figure 1.36.

3. **Start a new document.**

Click to display a blank document on your screen (Figure 1.37). You now have three documents open. Each of them resides in a separate Word window.

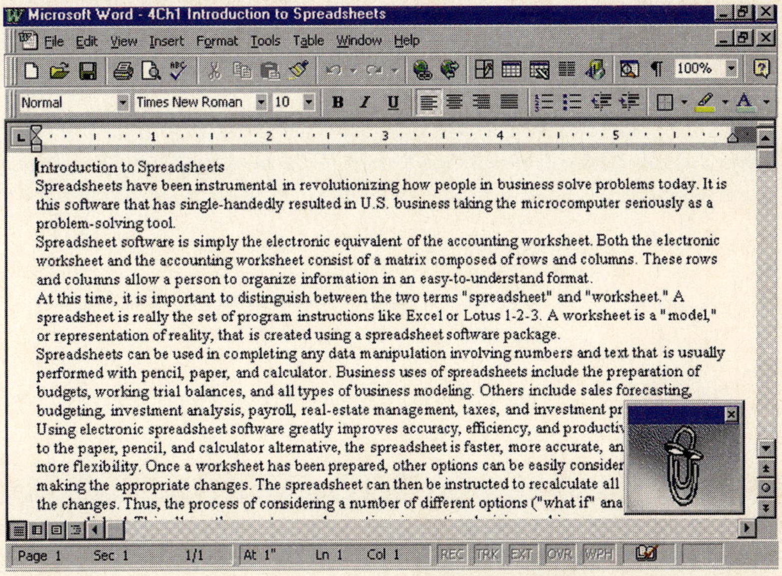

Figure 1.36
The Word window with the 4Ch1 Introduction to Spreadsheets document loaded.

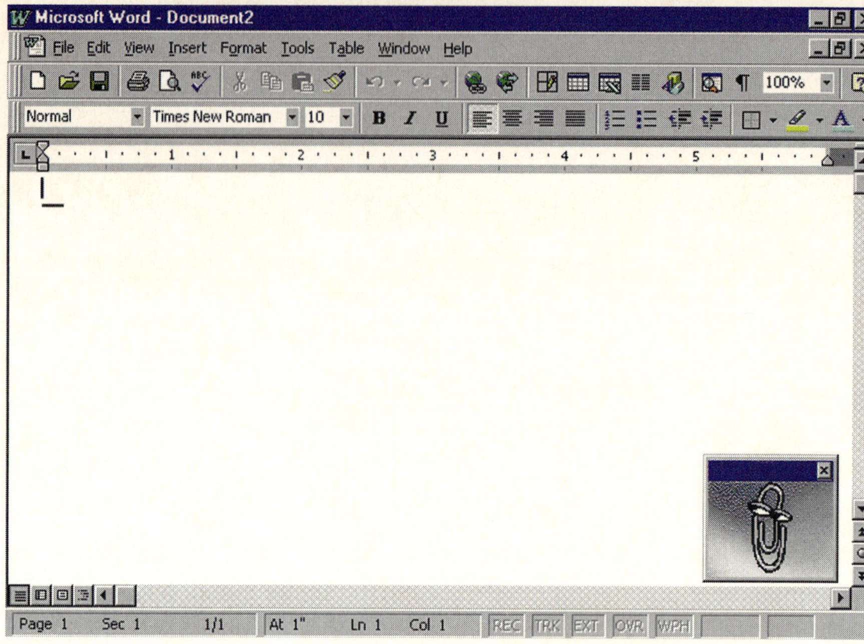

Figure 1.37
A blank document opened in Word.

4. **Verify the number of documents that you have opened.**

Window Click to display the Window menu (Figure 1.38). You should see the names of the two files you have just loaded as well as the name of the blank document (Document2).

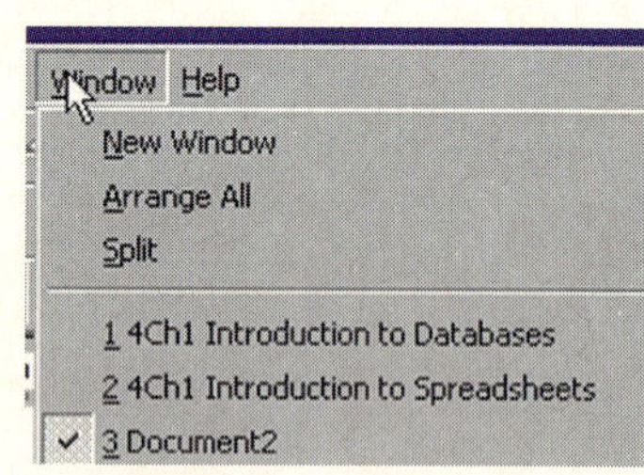

Figure 1.38
The Window menu with all open documents listed at the bottom.

4Ch1 Introduction to Databases Click this document name. You should now see this document displayed in the Word window.

Window Click to display the Window menu with its list of open files.

Document2 Click to return to the blank window.

5. **Enter one line of text in this blank document screen.**

Type: **This is a blank document that is to be saved to disk as a separate file.**

6. **Close the document and save it.**

 Click this button on the menu bar. The Office Assistant prompts you about saving the file (Figure 1.39).

Click to open the Save As dialog box shown in Figure 1.40. Notice that the default filename is the first line of the document. (This same dialog box would have appeared if you had clicked the Save button on the toolbar.)

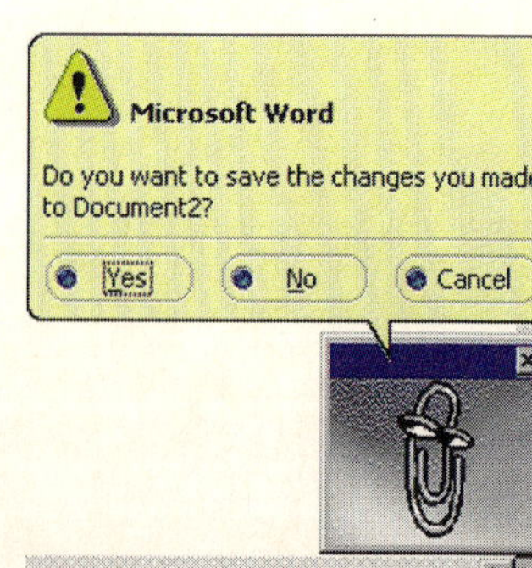

Figure 1.39
The Office Assistant prompting you about saving the document.

Type the name of the file: **M3Ch1 Sample Document**

Click to save the document. You should now see the Ch1 Introduction to Databases document.

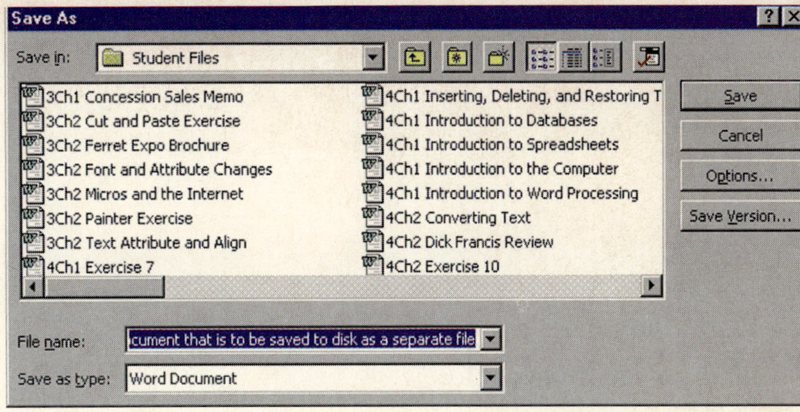

Figure 1.40
The Save As dialog box for saving an unnamed document.

7. **Use the Save As command to save another copy of the 4Ch1 Introduction to Databases document.**

File Click to open the File menu.

Save As. . . Click to open the Save As dialog box.

Type the new name of the document: **M3Ch1 Database Backup**

The Save As dialog box should look like Figure 1.41.

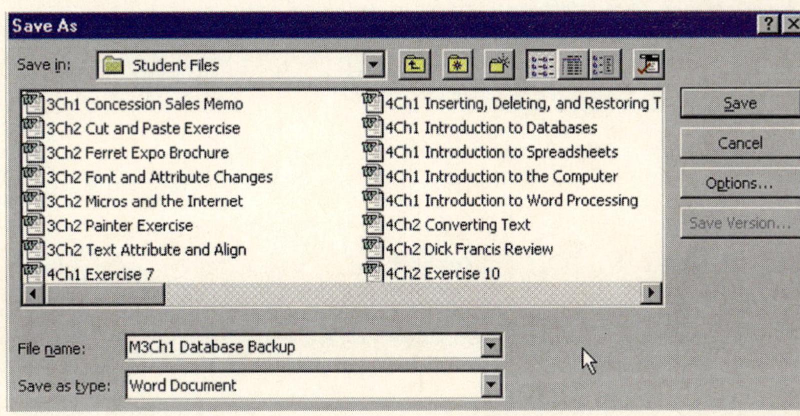

Figure 1.41
The completed Save As dialog box used to save a copy of the 4Ch1 Introduction to Database document under the name M3Ch1 Database Backup.

Click to save a copy of the document using the new name. Notice that the name of the document that appears in the title bar has changed to reflect the name specified in the Save As dialog box (Figure 1.42).

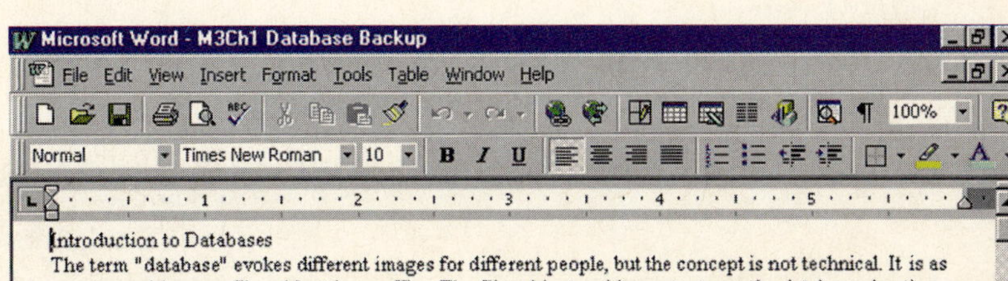

Figure 1.42
The newly specified document name appears in the title bar.

8. **If you have the IntelliMouse, experiment with the IntelliMouse commands contained in Table 1.2 to move around the document.**

9. **Exit the application.**

Click the Close button at the right end of the title bar. You should return to the Windows desktop.

Reinforcing the Exercise

1. You can close a document either by using the File, Close command sequence or by clicking the document's Close button.
2. If you issue a Close command for an unnamed document, the Save As dialog box appears when you indicate that that document is to be saved.
3. You can use the Save As command to create a copy of a document using another name.
4. You can use the New Document button on an application's toolbar to open a blank document.
5. You can use the Windows menu to switch from one open document to another.

PRINTING A DOCUMENT

File, Print, or 

Most Office applications provide two methods for printing a document: issuing the File, Print command sequence or clicking the Print button.

Using the File, Print Command Sequence

Issuing the File, Print command sequence opens the Print dialog box (Figure 1.43), which gives you control over how the document is to be printed.

The Printer box indicates which printer will be used by the Print Manager (you will typically use the Windows default printer). The Print what list box indicates what will be printed (the default is the entire document or workbook). The Page range box indicates how much of the document will be printed (the default is all). The Copies box indicates how many copies will be made. Once you have made your selections, click the OK button to send the document to the Print Manager.

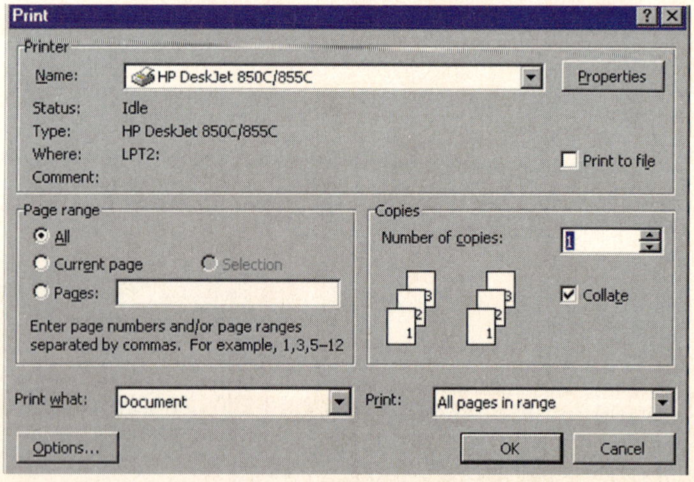

Figure 1.43
The Print dialog box for Word.

Using the Print Button 

When you click the Print button, the Office application that is open assumes that you want the entire document printed and immediately sends it to the Print Manager. No dialog box is displayed, so you cannot change any printing settings.

The Printer Icon

Note that, no matter which method you select for printing a document, a printer icon appears in the status bar as the document is being assembled for printing by the Office application. As each page is prepared, the page number appears beside the printer icon.

After the document has been assembled, a printer icon appears on the taskbar indicating that the document has been passed to the Print Manager. If you receive a printer error message, or if you want to check the status of the print job, double-click the printer icon on the taskbar to open the Print Manager window.

USING PRINT PREVIEW

File, Print Preview or 

Sometimes when you print a document using a software application, you are surprised by the difference between printed output and the on-screen display. Often, print features such as headers, footers, and page numbers do not appear on the screen, so it is often difficult to see whether these features have even been activated.

Each Office application has a **Print Preview feature** that you can use to solve this problem. You access Print Preview by issuing the File, Print Preview command sequence or by clicking the Print Preview button. A **Preview window** like that shown in Figure 1.44 appears.

When the text size is less than 100 percent, the text appears as simulated, or "greeked," text; that is, a representation of the text is used instead of the individual, readable characters. The Preview window does, however, display all elements of the document.

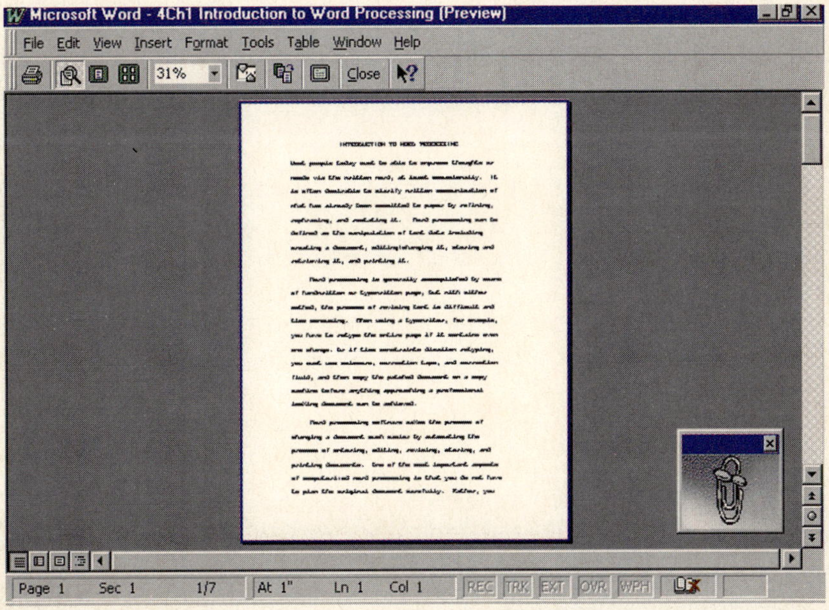

Figure 1.44
The Preview window for a Word document.

Manipulating the Previewed Document

A number of buttons appear at the top of the Preview window that you can use to manipulate the previewed document. These buttons are summarized in Table 1.4. The menu bar also appears in the Preview window, so you can issue commands from it to change the appearance of the previewed document.

Table 1.4 Preview Window Buttons

Button	Name of Button	Function
	Print	Sends the document immediately to the printer. No Print dialog box is displayed.
	Magnifier	Changes the pointer to a magnifying glass. Click the part of the document you want magnified. Click that part again to return it to its original size.
	One Page	Displays one page of the document at a time.
	Multiple Pages	Displays a menu that allows you to determine the number of pages to be displayed at one time.
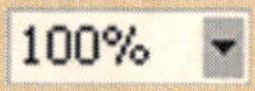	Zoom	Controls the size of the simulated text displayed in the Preview window. The Office default setting is typically used for this button.
	View Ruler	Activates the ruler for the previewed document. The ruler shows where the left and right margins are, along with any tab stops that have been included in the document.
	Shrink to Fit	Reduces the number of pages in a document by one by slightly changing the size of type used in the document.
	Full Screen	Hides most of the screen elements (menus, toolbars, and so forth) so that more of the document can be previewed.
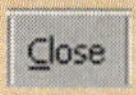	Close Preview	Closes the Preview window and returns to the application window.
	Context Sensitive Help	Click this to turn the pointer into a big question mark. When you now click a button or object, a help bubble appears explaining that item.

Hands-On Exercise: Previewing an Office Document

Isabel wants to use the Print Preview feature to demonstrate to several of the secretaries how easy it is to see exactly how a file will print. She also wants to demonstrate the effects of several of the Preview window buttons.

This exercise examines the Print Preview feature by using the Word document 4Ch1 Introduction to Word Processing. It assumes that you have Word started.

1. **Open the document.**

Open the Open dialog box by clicking this toolbar button. If necessary, select the drive and/or folder in the Look in list that contains your student files.

4Ch1 Introduction to Word Processing Double-click to load the document. Your screen should now look like that shown in Figure 1.45.

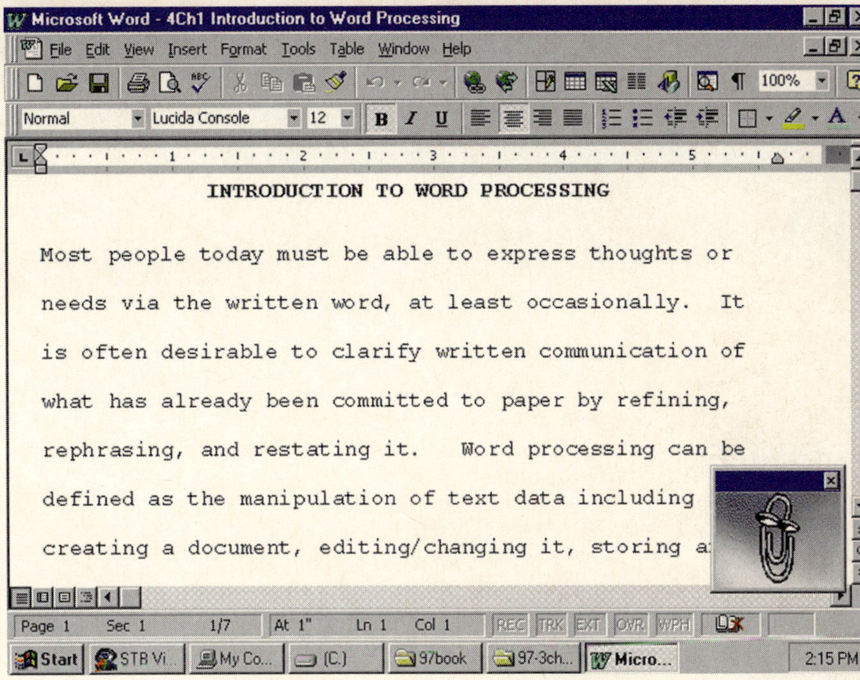

Figure 1.45
The 4Ch1 Introduction to Word Processing document loaded into Word.

2. **Open the Preview window.**

Click to see how the document will print (Figure 1.46).

3. **Indicate that the document is to be displayed with two pages across.**

Click to activate the Multiple Pages button menu (Figure 1.47).

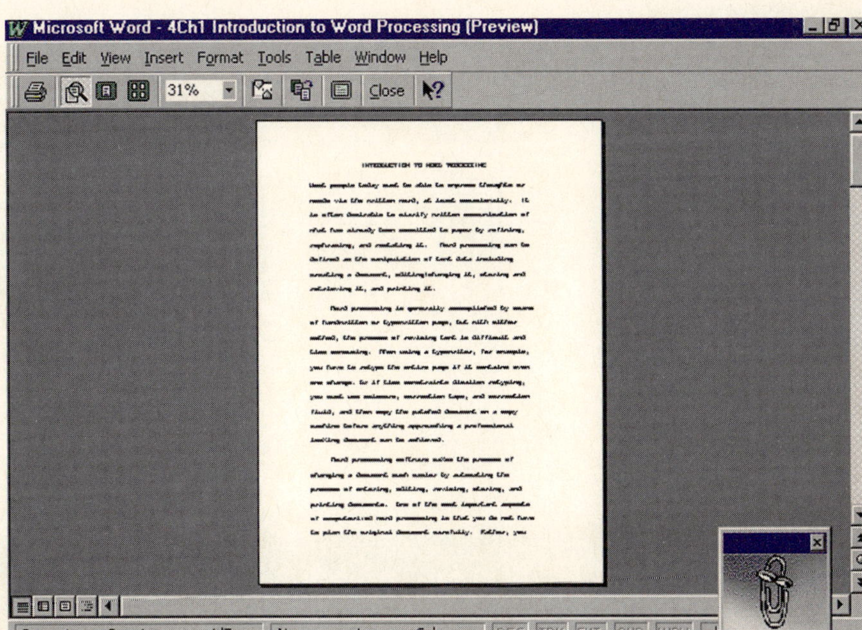

Figure 1.46
The document displayed in the Preview window.

Figure 1.47
The Multiple Pages button menu.

1 × 2 Pages Click the upper-left page (Figure 1.48).

Click Click below the scroll box on the scroll bar. The screen should now appear as shown in Figure 1.49.

4. Move around the document using keyboard commands.

 Click to return the display back to a single page.

(CTRL) + (HOME) Move to the beginning of the document.

(PGDN) (3 times) Press the Page Down key three times to go to page 4 of the document. The Preview window should now look like Figure 1.50.

Figure 1.48
The icon of the Multiple Pages button menu selected to display two pages across.

5. Magnify the document so you can read it.

 Click to use the magnifier. When you move the pointer over the document, it should appear like a magnifying glass (Figure 1.51).

Click Click the upper-left portion of the page to make the text readable (Figure 1.52).

 Click to display a single page of the document.

 Click to turn off the magnifier.

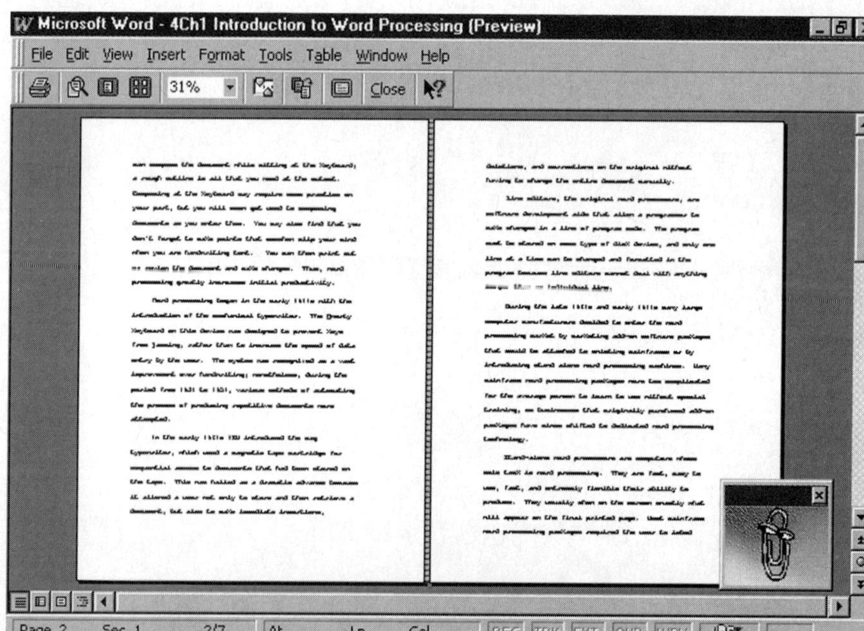

Figure 1.49
The document with two pages displayed across the Preview window.

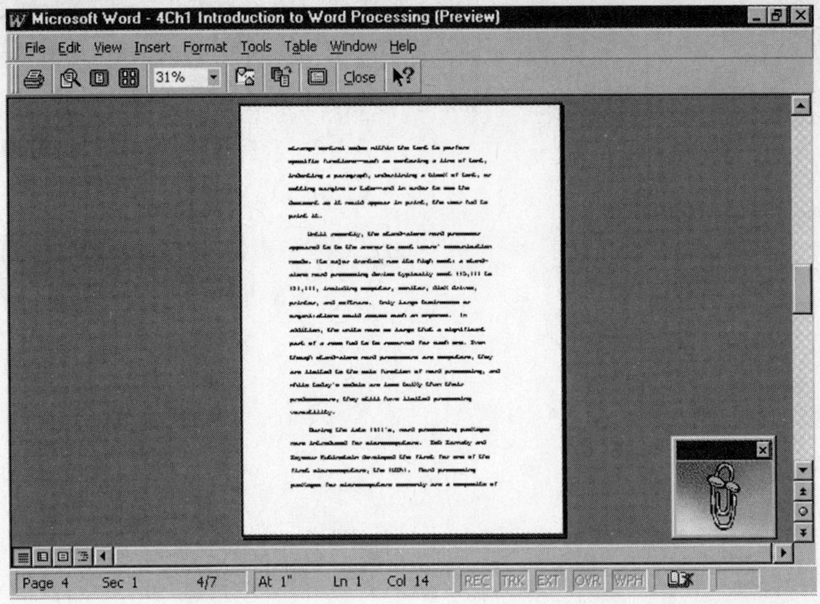

Figure 1.50
The document after you have moved forward three pages.

6. **Make as much of the page visible as possible by turning off other Preview window controls.**

View Click to open the View menu.

Full Screen Click to deactivate the menu bar and the status bar (Figure 1.53).

Notice that a menu appears controlling this feature.

Click the Close full screen button to reactivate the menu and status bars.

Figure 1.51
The magnifying feature of the Preview window with the mouse pointer changed to a magnifying glass.

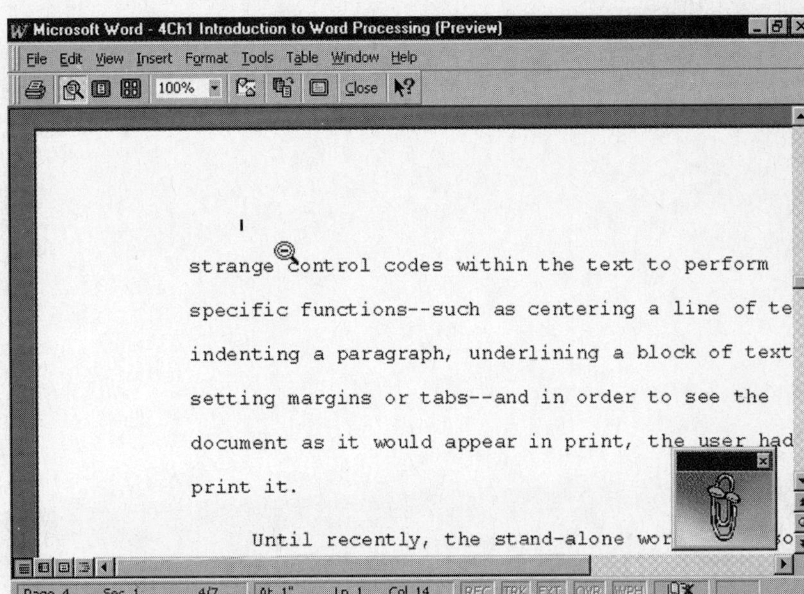

Figure 1.52
The text of the previewed page enlarged using the magnifier.

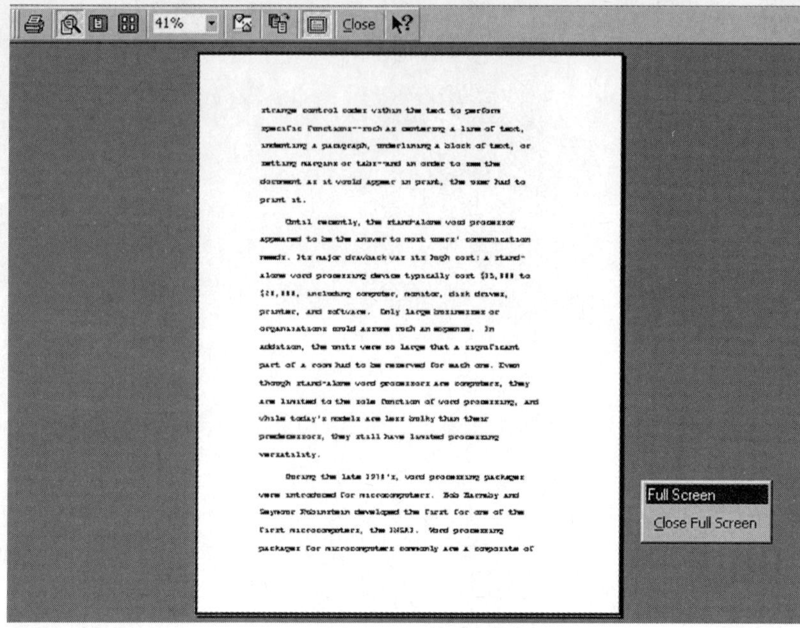

Figure 1.53
The Preview window with the Full Screen feature activated.

7. **Activate the ruler at the top of the previewed page.**

Click to activate the rulers and side of the previewed page (Figure 1.54).

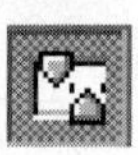

Click to deactivate the rulers of the previewed page.

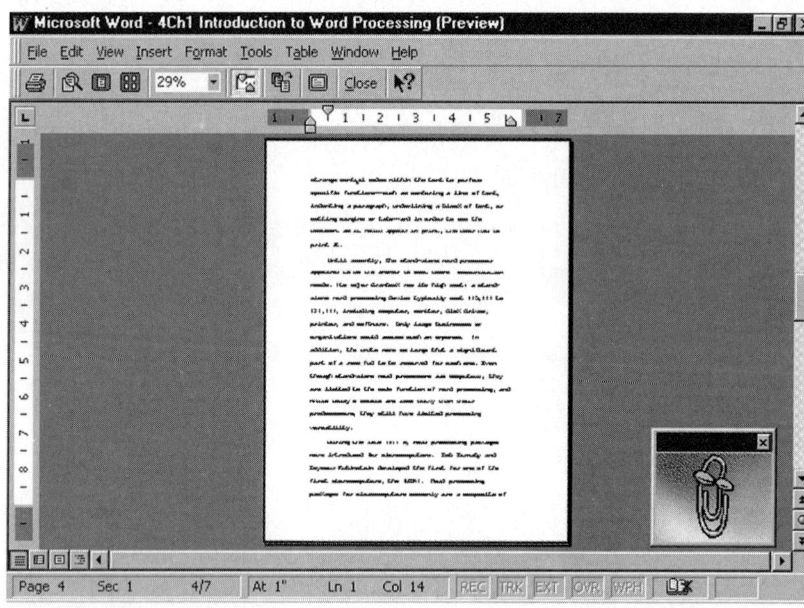

Figure 1.54
The Preview window with the ruler activated.

8. **Return to the Word document.**

Click the Close button of the Preview window toolbar to return to the Word document.

9. **Exit Word and close the document.**

Click the Close button in the Word title bar to return to the Windows desktop. If a dialog box appears prompting you about saving the document, click the No button.

Reinforcing the Exercise

1. You can use the Print Preview feature to see how a document will print without having to actually print it.
2. The Multiple Pages button allows you to determine how many pages you preview at one time.
3. The Magnifier button allows you to examine the actual text in a document.
4. The One Page button displays only one page of text at a time.
5. You can use keyboard commands to move around the previewed document.

OFFICE BINDERS

The **binder** is a new concept that was added to Office 95 and has been greatly expanded in Office 97. A binder holds copies of related electronic documents you have created in various Office applications. The documents always stay in the order in which you originally placed them until you move them by using an Office command. You can save, move, and print a binder as you would a single document.

To create a new binder, you click the Start button, then the New Office Document button, click the General tab, and then double-click Blank Binder. To open an existing binder, you can double-click that binder filename in the Open dialog box.

Beginning with Office 97, you can make changes to the documents you have assembled in a binder and have those changes reflected in the original document. A binder is a useful place to hold components of reports or presentations that you give frequently and need to get to easily.

Like other objects in Office 97, binders now have Internet support. You can save binders to the local disk or place them on the World Wide Web.

Hands-On Exercise: Examining an Office Binder

Isabel asked Janet, one of her employees, to put a spreadsheet containing concession sales data together with a memo to the staff. She is about to examine the binder that contains this information before she sends it to the other staff members.

1. **Open the binder.**

Activate the Start menu.

Activate the Open dialog box. Change the Look in box to drive A or the location where your student files are stored.

3Ch1 Concession Sales Open the 3Ch1 Concession Sales binder. The application associated with the first document in the binder starts automatically. In this case, the Word program starts and a memo document opens. Use the scroll bar at the right of the document to go to the beginning of the memo, as shown in Figure 1.55.

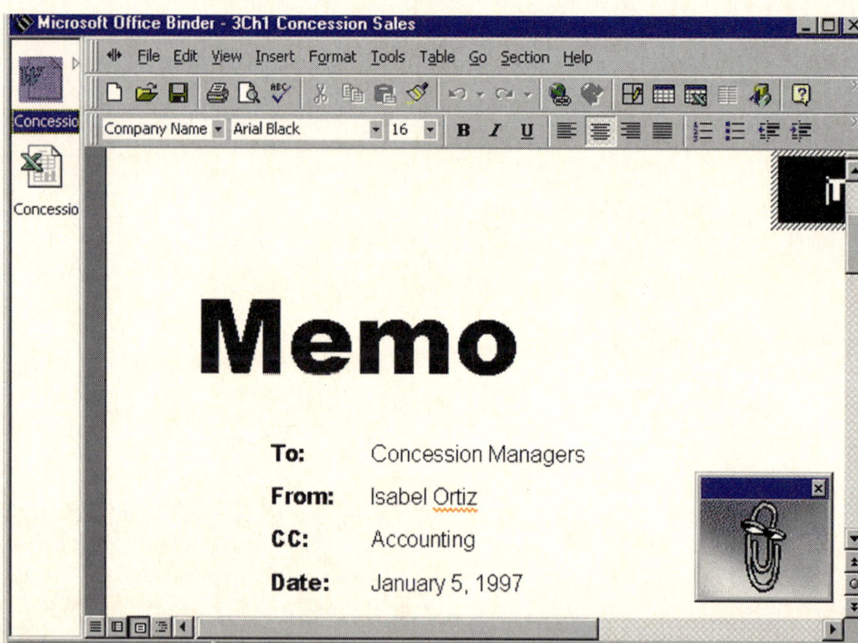

Figure 1.55
The memo document from the 3Ch1 Concession Sales binder.

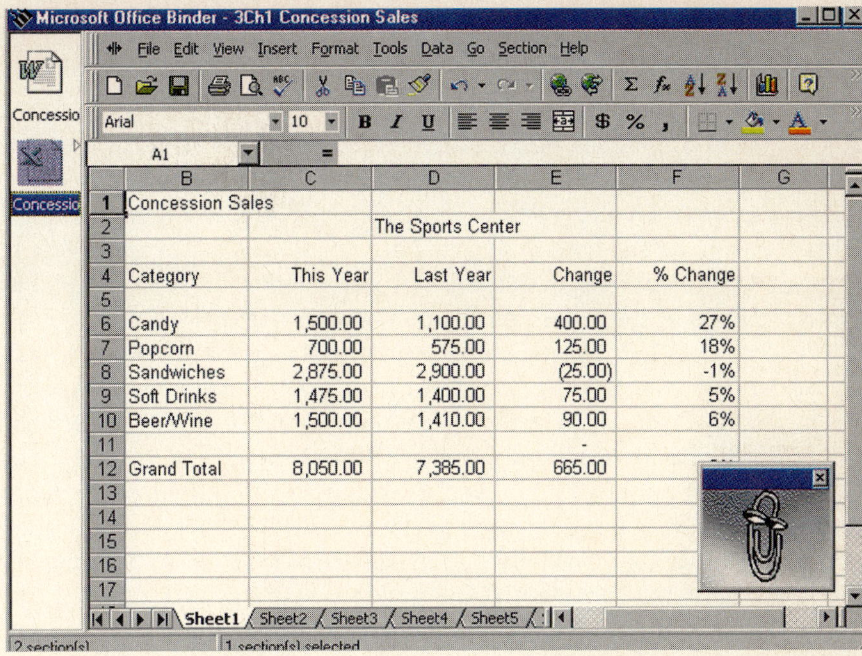

Figure 1.56
The Excel worksheet containing the year-to-date concession sales data.

Load the 3Ch1 Concession Sales worksheet (Figure 1.56).

Locate this button at the left end of the menu bar, and click to make the binder icons disappear.

Click to make the binder icons reappear.

2. **Print the memo and worksheet.**

File Click to open the File menu.

Print Binder . . . Click to open the Print Binder dialog box.

Click to print the documents in the binder.

3. **Close the binder**

Click the Close button. A dialog box opens, asking if you want to save changes.

Click to indicate that you do not want to save changes. You return to the Windows desktop.

Reinforcing the Exercise

1. Binders hold copies of related documents. Any changes you make to a document in a binder also appear in the original document.
2. When you open a document in a binder, its corresponding application also opens.

SESSION REVIEW

Microsoft Office is a suite of software applications designed to work together, sharing data using the same commands. Because all five applications in the suite use a number of similar commands, Office is easy to learn and use. Office is also Web aware.

You use the Open dialog to load documents into the application window. In the Open dialog box, you use the Look in selection box to choose the drive or folder that contains the documents you want to open. The Open dialog box also provides several buttons that allow you to control how document information appears in the dialog box.

If you do not know the name of a document, but you know a key word or phrase, you can use the Open dialog box to search for and display documents containing that text.

Use the New icon on an application toolbar to start a new document. Using Start, or New Office document commands, you will have the option of starting a blank document or using an existing template. A template is a prewritten document that you can modify.

You can use the Close command to close a document so you can start another. If you have made changes to a previously unsaved document, a dialog box appears, prompting you about saving the document. If you decide to save the file for the first time, a Save As dialog box appears, prompting you to enter a name for the file.

Use the Save command to periodically save your document. Use the Save As command if you want to save the document using a different name.

You can print a document by using the Print dialog box or by clicking the Print button on an application toolbar. The Print dialog box gives you control over how a document is printed, whereas the Print button sends the document directly to the printer using existing (default or already defined) print options.

The Print Preview command allows you to see how a document will appear when it is printed. Some document features that may not be visible on-screen are displayed in the Preview window. A number of buttons in the Preview window allow you to control how the document is displayed.

A binder is a storage device for holding related documents created in various Office applications. You can change a document stored in a binder. A presentation containing numerous files is an example of a good use of binders.

KEY TERMS AND CONCEPTS

binder 3–29
IntelliMouse 3–3
Office Assistant 3–4
Preview window 3–23
Print Preview feature 3–23
Shortcut bar 3–4
shortcut icon 3–3
suite 3–2
Web aware 3–3

SESSION QUIZ

Multiple Choice

1. Which of the following does not result in a Save command being executed?
   a. File, Exit
   b. Clicking the Close button
   c. File, Close
   d. All of these can result in the execution of a Save command

2. Which of the following is not an option in the Print dialog box?
   a. Print a range of pages
   b. Print only the current page or selection
   c. Change the font
   d. All of these are options in the Print dialog box
3. Which of the following commands always invokes a dialog box?
   a. File, Save
   b. Save button
   c. File, Print
   d. Print button
4. Which of the following buttons does not appear in the Open dialog box?
   a. Properties
   b. Preview
   c. Print
   d. Details
   e. All of the above buttons
5. Which of the following commands does not open a dialog box?
   a. File, Open
   b. File, Save As
   c. File, Print
   d. File, Save

True/False

6. If you really mess up a file you are editing, the safest thing to do is issue a Close command without saving changes.
7. An advantage of using Office is that data can easily be passed from one Office application to another.
8. The Save As dialog box can be used to make a copy of a document.
9. The Print button, when clicked, automatically displays the Print dialog box.
10. Print Preview allows you to see a document exactly as it will be printed.

SESSION REVIEW EXERCISES

1. Define or describe each of the following:
   a. magnifier
   b. binder
   c. Print Preview
2. The long, narrow bar that may appear on the title bar is called the ______________ bar.
3. From the desktop, you can open the Open dialog box by clicking the Open Office Document option in the ______________ menu.
4. The ______________ ______________ command sequence issued in a Windows application opens a new file, not an existing one.

5. Clicking the ______________ button of a document window lets you exit the document being edited or created.
6. When you are working with large documents, it is a good idea to use the ______________ command every 10 to 15 minutes.
7. The command sequence to invoke Print Preview is ______________, ______________.
8. An Office application can be started and loaded by double-clicking a(n) ______________ document in the Open dialog box.
9. You use the ______________ ______________ list box of the Open dialog box to change the drive or folder used for accessing documents.
10. In the Open dialog box, you can examine the beginning of a specific document by clicking the ______________ button.
11. Clicking the ______________ button in the Open dialog box lets you see who is the author of the document, the size of the document, and so forth.
12. You can also perform file maintenance tasks on selected documents and files in the Open dialog box by clicking the ______________ mouse button to invoke the context menu.
13. Once you have entered criteria for performing a search using the Open dialog box, you can execute the search by clicking the ______________ ______________ button.
14. You can prepare any document for placement on the World Wide Web by using the File, ______________ ______________ command sequence.
15. The ______________ button in the Preview window allows you to actually read a portion of the previewed document.
16. The ______________ ______________ is a help feature that takes the form of an animated character on-screen.
17. The ______________ dialog box allows you to control which part of a document is printed.
18. The File, ______________ ______________ command sequence allows you to see exactly how a document will print.
19. A(n) ______________ allows you to store documents together that are used for a related task.
20. The ______________ button in an application toolbar always starts a blank document.

COMPUTER EXERCISES

1. Open the Open dialog box using the Open Office Document menu entry of the Start menu. Set the Look in list box to the location where your data files are stored. All files should be displayed.
   a. Use the Preview button to examine five different documents.
   b. Use the Property button to examine five other files.
   c. Use the Details button to display more information on each document.
   d. Return the display back to List.
   e. Search for any files that contain the word *programming*.

2. Use the My Computer window to go to the location of your student files. Practice starting Office applications by double-clicking associated files.
3. Open the 4Ch 1Purchasing a Computer Word document.
   a. Use the Print Preview command to display the document six pages at a time.
   b. Print the first page of the document.
   c. Close the document.
4. Choose the New Office Document menu option on the Start menu. Select the Letters & Faxes tab.
   a. Double-click the Elegant Letter template.
   b. Fill in the blanks to create the document.
   c. Leave the body of the letter as is.
   d. Print the document.
   e. Use the Save As command to save the document with your name at the end of the original document name (M3Ch1 Elegant Letter - Your Name).
5. Start Word and then perform the following tasks:
   a. Open four Word documents.
   b. Open a new document.
   c. Use the Windows menu to switch from one document to the other.
6. Use the Open dialog box to find any files that contain the word *delete.*
   a. Open the first file with the searched-for value.
   b. Print the document.
   c. Exit without saving the document.
7. Open a file and practice closing it using the commands listed here. Make any type of change to the document. Notice how each command functions a little differently. When you are queried about saving the file, always click the No button.
   a. Invoke the File, Close command sequence.
   b. Click the document's Close button (which appears on the menu bar).
   c. Click the application's Close button (which appears on the title bar).
8. Open the 4Ch 1Purchasing a Computer document. Perform the following print tasks:
   a. Print the first page of the document.
   b. Print the third and fourth pages using one Print command.
   c. Close the document without saving any changes you might have made.
9. Open the 4Ch 1Purchasing a Computer document, and practice using the Print Preview command by performing the following tasks:
   a. Practice using the Multiple Pages button by displaying various numbers of pages in the Preview window.
   b. Practice using the magnifier to make the previewed text readable.
   c. Set the Preview window to full screen mode. Then return the screen to the regular display mode.
   d. Set Print Preview to One Page mode.
   e. Exit Print Preview.
   f. Close the document without saving any changes you might have made.

10. Start Excel and load an Excel document.
    a. Use the File, Print command sequence to open the Print dialog box. Examine this dialog box for any differences with the Word Print dialog box. Print the document.
    b. Invoke Print Preview in Excel. Use the Zoom command to examine the document. Click the Print button to print the document.
    c. Leave Excel without saving any changes you might have made.

INTERNET EXERCISES

Internet Activities

1. Check out some games being marketed by Microsoft.
    a. Use your browser to visit the Microsoft Web site (http://microsoft.com).
    b. Examine the appropriate software/games link.
    c. Download a free trial version of a game if you would like.
2. Find out more about the Binder feature of Office 97.
    a. Use your browser to visit the Microsoft Web site (http://microsoft.com).
    b. Activate the Search feature by clicking the Search button at the top of the Microsoft Web page.
    c. Make certain that only the microsoft.com selection button is activated when you get to the Search page (this will search only the Microsoft site).
    d. In the Search text box, enter the work *Binder*.
    e. Examine any Web pages that might be of interest to you.
    f. Print one Web page.

SESSION 2

More Common Office Commands

After completing this session, you should be able to:

- Use the Office Help feature
- Manually navigate through an Office document
- Edit a document
- Use taskbar commands common to Office applications
- Use the Format Painter to apply attributes of existing text to other text
- Use the Office Art feature to draw lines and shapes and embed them in documents
- Use the WordArt feature to create interesting shapes from text.

Isabel wants to examine the Help feature of the Office software suite. She also wants to get acquainted with the commands commonly used in Office applications for moving around documents.

One of Isabel's employees needs help in creating a brochure announcing an upcoming event at the Civic Arena that his organization is sponsoring. He has the basic information for the event in a word processing file and wants Isabel's help in making the brochure more attractive by adding graphics.

OFFICE HELP FEATURE Help, Contents and Index

As discussed in Session 1 of this module, the Office Assistant is one of the primary sources of help in any Office application. Office applications also offer the same types of Help offered by Windows (see Module 1: Windows 95, Session 1). ToolTips, the What's This button, ScreenTips, and the Help dialog box all function the same in both programs.

You access the Office Help feature from the Help Topics dialog box, as you do in Windows. As shown in Figures 2.1, 2.2, and 2.3, the Contents tab, Index tab, and Find tab in the Excel Help Topics dialog box all perform the same function as in Windows.

If you have any questions about using the Help feature, refer to Module 1: Windows 95.

On Your Own

Practice using the Help feature of Microsoft Office applications.

- Open Word and look up the following topics:
  Printing, Bold, Undo, Spell
- Open Excel and look up the same topics.

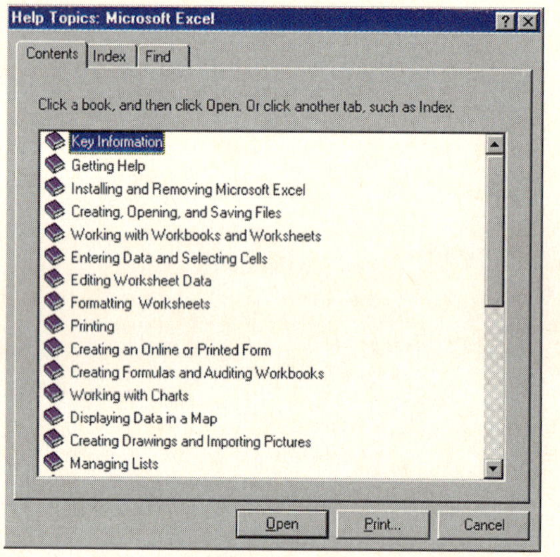

Figure 2.1
The Contents tab of the Excel Help dialog box.

MOVING AROUND AN OFFICE DOCUMENT

Once you have opened an Office document, you are not restricted to the mouse for moving around a document. You can also use a number of common keyboard commands to position the insertion point without moving your hands from the keyboard (Table 2.1). You can issue these commands by using the keys on the ten-key number pad, or by using the arrow keys and other positioning keys normally found between the ten-key pad and the alphanumeric portion of the keyboard.

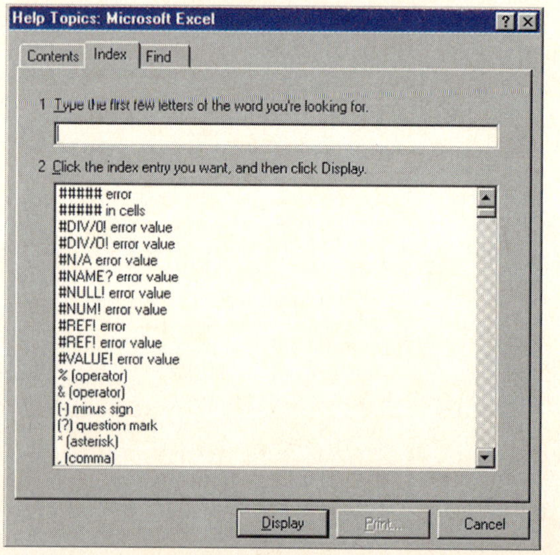

Figure 2.2
The Index tab of the Excel Help dialog box.

Hands-On Exercise: Moving Within a Document

This exercise requires you to be at the Windows desktop.

1. **Start Word.**
2. **Open the 4Ch2 Introduction to Word Processing document (Figure 2.4).**

3. **Go to the end of the document.**

   CTRL + END — Press these keys to move to the end of the document. Your screen should look like the one shown in Figure 2.5.

   CTRL + HOME — Press these keys to move back to the beginning of the document. Your document should again look like the one shown in Figure 2.4.

4. **Use the positioning commands from Table 2.1 to move about the document.**
5. **When you are finished, click the Close button on the application title bar to exit Word without saving any changes to the document.**
6. **Start Excel and open any Excel document.** Use the positioning commands from Table 2.1 to move about the document.
7. **Click the Close button of the application title bar to exit Excel without saving the document.**

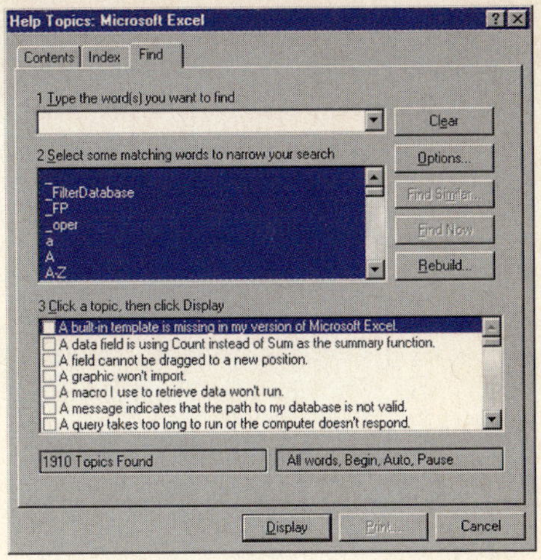

Figure 2.3
The Find tab of the Excel Help dialog box.

Table 2.1 Keys for Moving Around a Document

Key	Purpose
←	Move to the left one character or column
→	Move to the right one character or column
↑	Move up one line
↓	Move down one line
PGUP	Move up one screen
PGDN	Move down one screen
CTRL + HOME	Move to the beginning of the document
CTRL + END	Move to the end of the document

Reinforcing the Exercise

1. Office applications use a number of common positioning commands.
2. You can move immediately to the beginning or end of a document.
3. A number of other types of positioning commands allow you to move through the text a character, line, or screen at a time.
4. As each application is introduced in successive sessions, more positioning commands found only in that application will be introduced.

MAKING CHANGES TO A DOCUMENT

Making changes to a document is a process called editing. **Editing** can involve correcting misspelled words, inserting new words, and deleting text.

The AutoCorrect Feature

All Office applications use a feature called **AutoCorrect** that automatically checks for commonly misspelled words and corrects those misspellings as you enter text in a document. For example, if you enter *teh* for the word *the* the Office application will automatically correct that misspelling for you.

In addition to correcting spelling errors, AutoCorrect creates special symbols for you when you enter certain characters from the keyboard (Table 2.2).

When you invoke the Tools, AutoCorrect command sequence, the dialog box shown in Figure 2.6 opens. The AutoCorrect dialog box has four tabs. The AutoCorrect tab, which opens by default, allows you to add words to AutoCorrect's list of automatically corrected words.

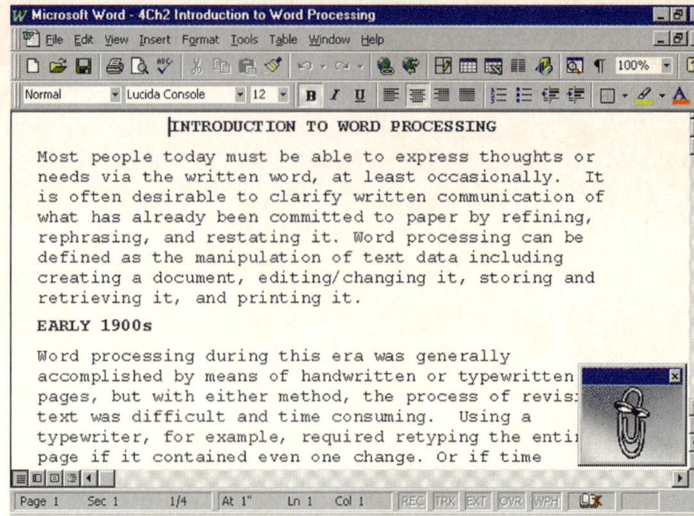

Figure 2.4
The 4Ch2 Introduction to Word Processing document.

At the top of the AutoCorrect tab are check boxes that indicate the type of corrections AutoCorrect will make. At the bottom of the AutoCorrect tab is a two-column word list box. On the left side of this list box are the incorrect spellings that are automatically detected; on the right side of the list box are the correct spellings. To add a word to this list box, enter the incorrect spelling in the Replace text box, enter the correct spelling in the With text box, and then click the Add button. Click the OK button to return to the Office application. Now whenever you type that misspelling, AutoCorrect will correct it for you.

If you are using Word, Office provides you with one more piece of help. If you enter a word that is not contained in the

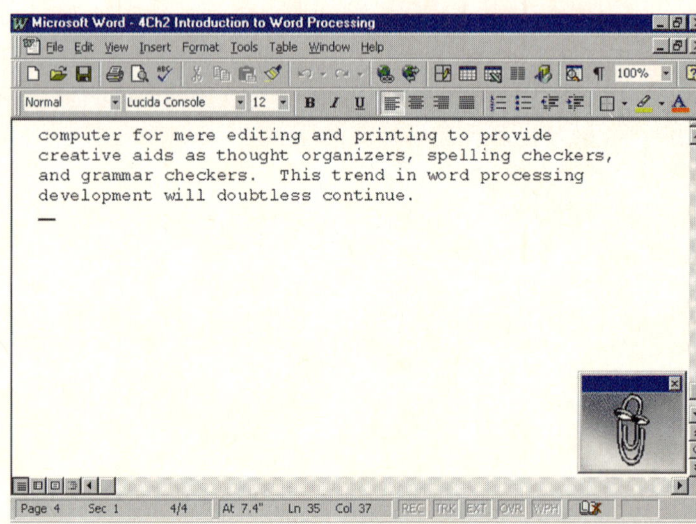

Figure 2.5
The 4Ch2 Introduction to Word Processing document with the insertion point moved to the last page.

Table 2.2 Some Special Characters Created by AutoCorrect

Character Sequence	Special Character Created*
(c)	©
(r)	®
(tm)	™
<--	←
<==	⬅

*To see other characters, invoke the Tools, AutoCorrect command sequence and examine the list box at the bottom of the AutoCorrect dialog box.

AutoCorrect word list nor in the Office dictionary, a ragged red line appears under the word, indicating that it may be misspelled. (The word may be correctly spelled but just not contained in the dictionary.) To correct one of these misspellings, right-click the mouse on the word with the red wavy line. A context menu appears with suggested corrections (Figure 2.7).

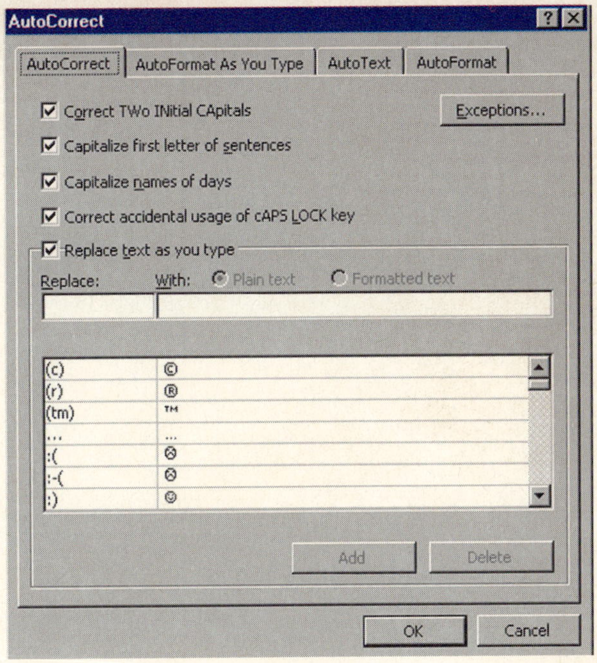

Figure 2.6
The AutoCorrect dialog box.

Checking Grammar

Office applications also have the ability to automatically check the grammar of a document as you enter it. If you make a subject-verb agreement error, use the passive voice, or use a sentence that is too long, the grammar checker will place a wavy green line under the suspect text.

To examine one of these grammar flags, right-click the mouse on the words with the green wavy line, and a context menu appears with suggested corrections (Figure 2.8). Clicking the Grammar option of the context menu generates a series of Help items, as shown in Figure 2.9.

Inserting Text

Office applications default to Insert mode. **Insert mode** moves existing text in a document to the right when new characters are added. **Overwrite mode** replaces existing characters with characters that you enter from the keyboard. Because Overwrite mode is rarely needed by most Office users, it is not available unless it was activated at installation. When Overwrite mode is activated, pressing (INS) switches back and forth between Insert and Overwrite mode.

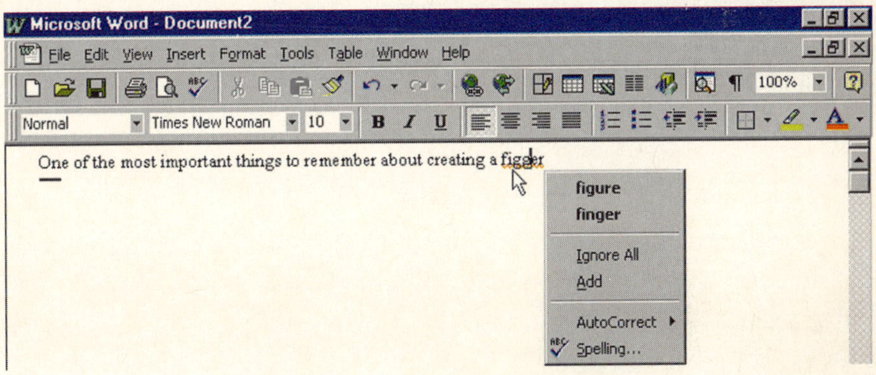

Figure 2.7
A misspelled word marked by a wavy red line, and the context menu suggesting a correct spelling.

Deleting Text

You can delete text in all Office applications by first using the mouse to select the text to be deleted and then pressing (BKSP) or (DEL) to delete the text. As you will see in the next part of this session, if you erroneously delete text, you can click the Undo button to restore the deleted text.

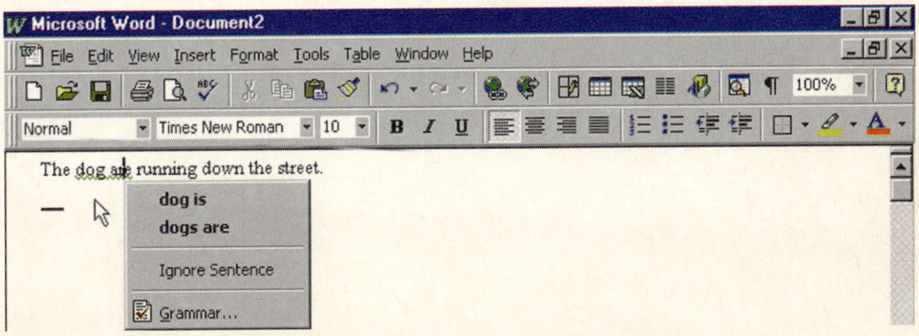

Figure 2.8
A sentence with a subject-verb agreement problem.

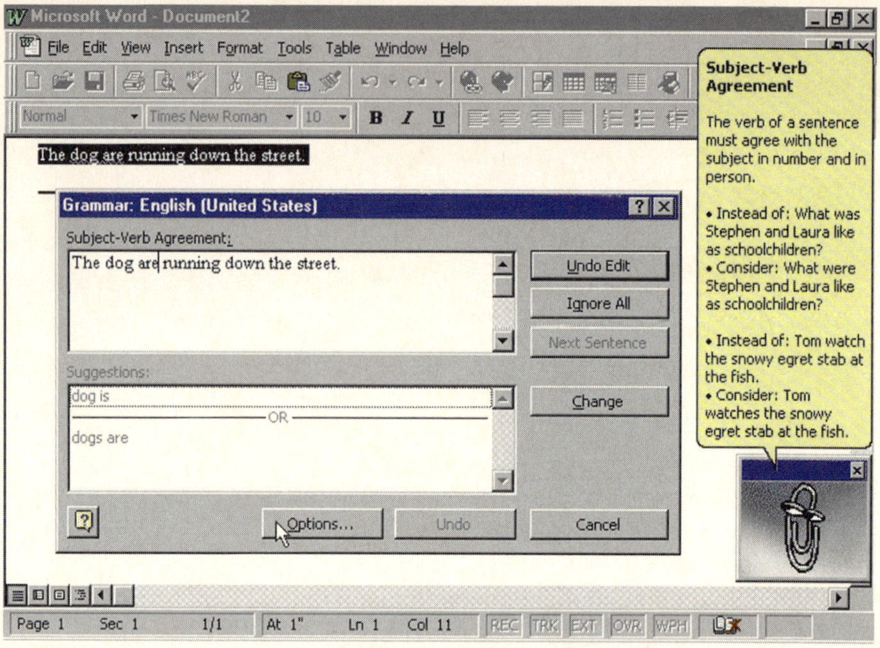

Figure 2.9
Additional help appears when you click on the Grammar option of the context menu.

You can also delete text one character at a time. Use the (DEL) key to delete the character at the insertion point. Use the (BKSP) key to delete the character to the left of the insertion point.

Hands-On Exercise: Using AutoCorrect, Spelling, and Insert Commands

This exercise requires you to have Word started and a blank document open. If necessary click the New button to open a blank document.

1. **Enter the text exactly as displayed in Figure 2.10.** As you are entering the text, try to misspell the word *the*. Be sure to press (ENTER) at the end of the second line. You should see several words with wavy red lines and one wavy green line.

Correcct Right-click the first word with a wavy red line. The context menu with spelling suggestions appears as shown in Figure 2.11.

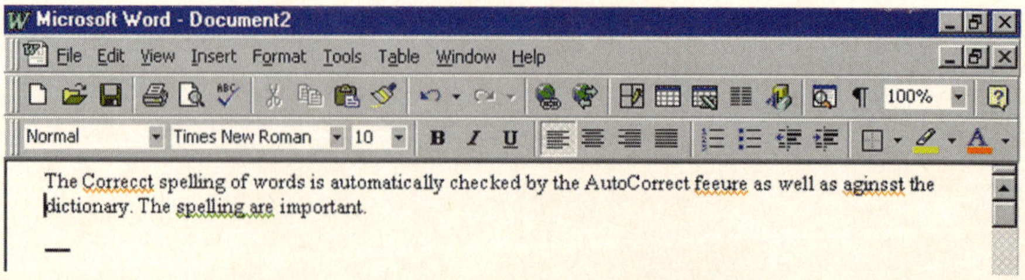

Figure 2.10
The document to be entered with misspelled words.

correct Click the correct spelling of the suspect word. The context menu disappears. Correct the capitalization.

feeure Right-click this word. Notice that the speller cannot find an appropriate correction for this word. You will have to change the word to *feature.* Continue until all suspect words with wavy red lines are corrected.

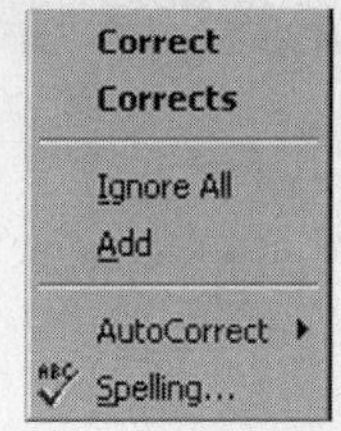

Figure 2.11
The context menu with boldfaced suggestions for the misspelled word *Correcct.*

2. **Correct the grammar error in the second sentence.** In the grammar context menu, indicate that the verb is to be singular (Figure 2.12).

3. **Move to the end of the document.**

(CTRL) + (END) Press these keys to move to the end of the document. The insertion point should be at the beginning of the blank line.

4. **Press (ENTER) ten times to add blank lines to your document.** Move back to the line just below the text you just entered. You are now going to examine a number of other features offered by AutoCorrect.

Figure 2.12
The context menu with corrections for the grammar error.

Type: **THe** When you type this word, be certain to enter a trailing space. Word immediately corrects the capitalization.

(ENTER) Press to move to the next line.

Type: **agian** Include a trailing space. Again, Word immediately corrects the misspelling.

(ENTER) Press to move to the next line.

Type: **:-)** Word immediately replaces these characters with a smiling face (☺).

(ENTER) Press to move to the next line.

Type: --> Word immediately replaces these characters with an arrow: →

(ENTER) Press to move to the next line.

Type: **(c)** You should now see the copyright symbol (©).

(ENTER) Press to move to the next line.

5. **Reverse the last action taken by AutoCorrect.** Suppose you want to leave your characters as they were before AutoCorrect changed them. Clicking the Undo button reverses the AutoCorrect change.

Type: <-- Word immediately changes this entry to ←.

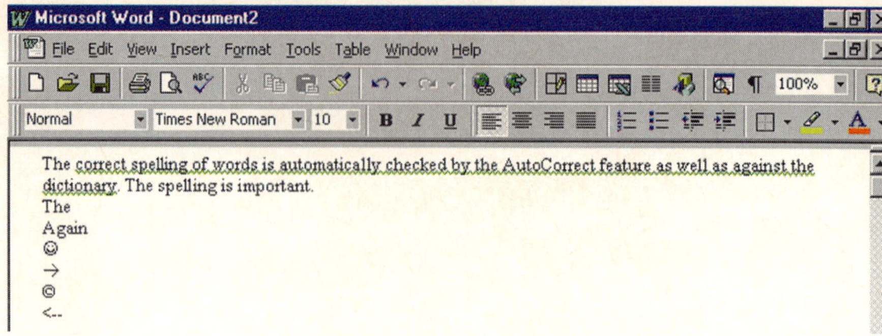

Figure 2.13
The Word document with several special characters added by the AutoCorrect feature.

Click the arrow portion of the Undo button. The left arrow returns to the characters <--. Your screen should now look like that shown in Figure 2.13.

6. **Examine the AutoCorrect dialog box.**

Tools	Click to activate the Tools pull-down menu.
AutoCorrect. . .	Click to activate the AutoCorrect dialog box shown in Figure 2.14. The special characters created by AutoCorrect using typed characters appear at the top of the list box.
Click	Click under the scroll box to see the next group of characters. Continue until you get to the list of words that AutoCorrect automatically corrects. Explore this feature as long as you like.

Click to return to Word when you are finished with your examination.

7. **Type three single underlines to create a border line.** This feature is not connected with AutoCorrect but is automatically performed by Word.

(↓)	Press the down arrow key to move to the next line.
Type: ---	by pressing the dash key three times with (SHIFT) held down. An underscore line now appears.
(↓)	Press the down arrow key to move to the next line. Notice that nothing happens in the line.

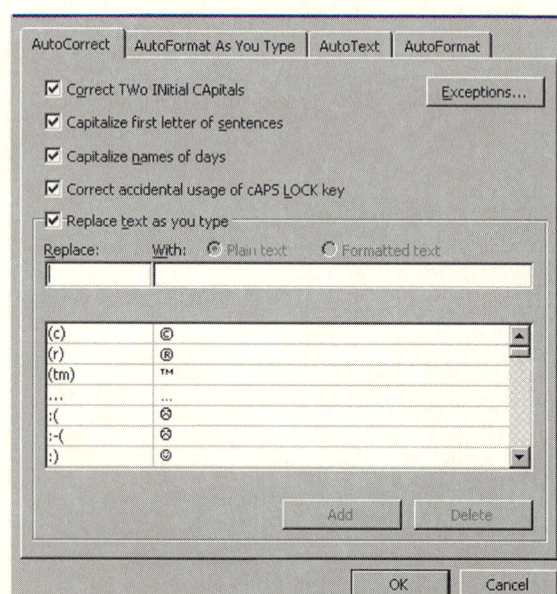

Figure 2.14
The AutoCorrect dialog box with the AutoCorrect tab showing the characters that this feature automatically generates in the right portion of the list box.

Type: --- by pressing the dash key three times with SHIFT held down. An underscore line again appears.

ENTER Press to create a thick black line. You may also get a message from the Office Assistant like that shown in Figure 2.15. If this does appear, click the Yes button. If you don't want the black line, you can click the Cancel button. Click Cancel to close the Office Assistant.

Click to return the document back to its prior state.

8. Delete a word.

CTRL + HOME Press to move to the beginning of the document.

DEL Press three times to delete the word *The*.

9. Restore the word *The* to the document a character at a time.

Click the Undo button. The last character deleted, *e*, appears.

Click the rounded arrow of the Undo button twice to make the *h* and *T* characters appear.

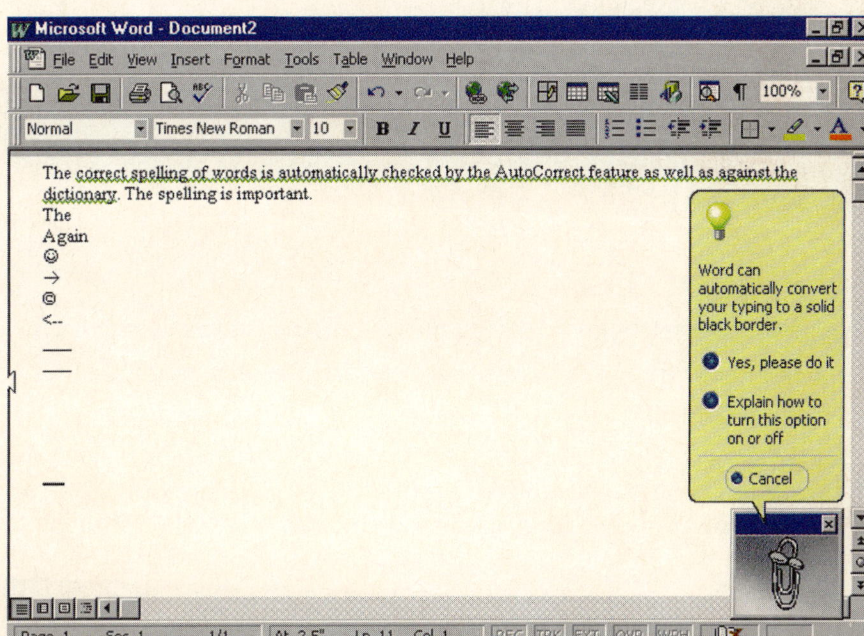

Figure 2.15
The Office Assistant's message about the automatically generated line.

10. Insert a word before the word *dictionary*.

Click	Click before the *d* of the word *dictionary* to move the insertion point to that location.
Type: **internal**	This word appears before the word *dictionary.* Be sure to include a space after the word *internal.*

11. Save the document.

File	Click to open the File menu.
Save	Click to open the Save As dialog box.

Type the filename: **M3Ch2 AutoCorrect Exercise**

Save the document to disk.

Click the document's Close button at the right of the menu bar to close it.

Reinforcing the Exercise

1. The AutoCorrect feature automatically corrects a number of misspelled words.
2. AutoCorrect also turns many typed character sequences into special characters on-screen.
3. To change a special character back to its original form, click the Undo button.
4. Text can be deleted using DEL.
5. Deleted text can be restored using the Undo button.
6. AutoCorrect automatically adds lines when you enter three dash or three underline characters and then press ENTER.
7. You can delete lines that were added automatically by clicking the Undo button.

USING COMMON TOOLBAR ELEMENTS

All Office software applications make extensive use of toolbars. A toolbar permits you to click buttons that contain little pictures representing tasks to be performed. Toolbars save you having to move through the various menu structures to access a commonly used command. The buttons on the toolbar vary with the software features that are active.

You can display and control different toolbars in any application using the View, Toolbars command sequence. This sequence invokes a Toolbars pull-down menu like that shown in Figure 2.16. Once the pull-down menu is displayed, you can activate the desired toolbar to use for this software application. Already activated toolbars appear with a checkmark by them.

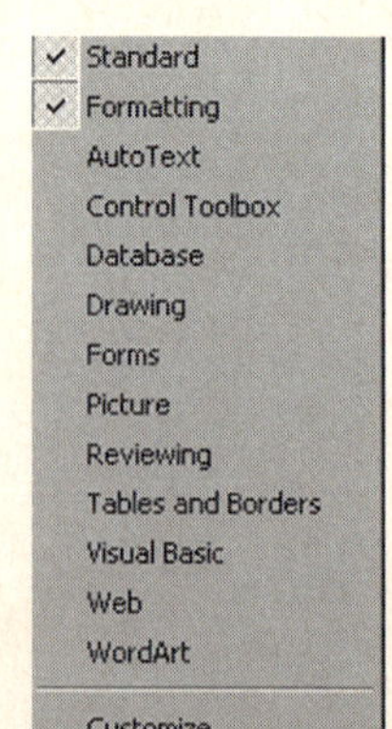

Figure 2.16
The Toolbars pull-down menu in Word controls which toolbars appear on the screen.

Each Office application typically appears with the Standard and Formatting toolbars active. The Office applications share a number of common toolbar button groups for performing common tasks. Once you understand the use of a group of buttons in one application, you can apply this knowledge to the buttons in other software applications.

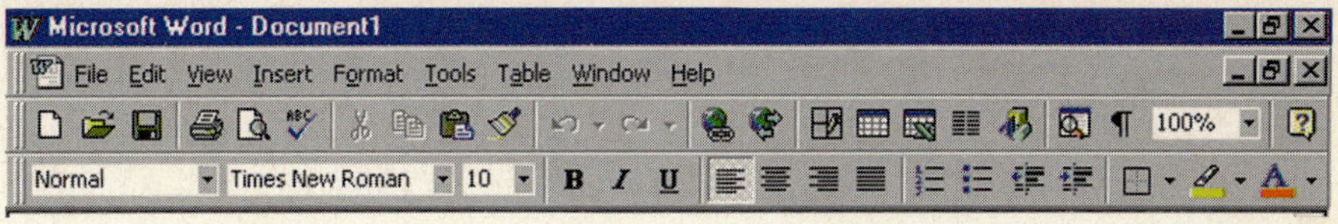

Figure 2.17
The Standard and Formatting toolbars for Word.

Figures 2.17 to 2.20 illustrate the toolbars for four Office applications. Figure 2.17 shows the toolbars for Word. The top toolbar (under the menu bar) is the Standard toolbar, and the toolbar underneath it is the Formatting toolbar. Figure 2.18 shows the Excel Standard (top) and Formatting (bottom) toolbars. Figure 2.19 shows the PowerPoint Standard (top) and Formatting (bottom) toolbars. Figure 2.20 shows the Access window with its single Standard toolbar.

Toolbar buttons are grouped together according to their use. Groups of buttons include file task buttons, printing and spelling buttons, text attribute buttons, font control buttons, the Cut and Paste buttons, the Undo and Redo buttons, and alignment buttons. You will be examining each of these groups of icons, along with the Format Painter, in the following sections.

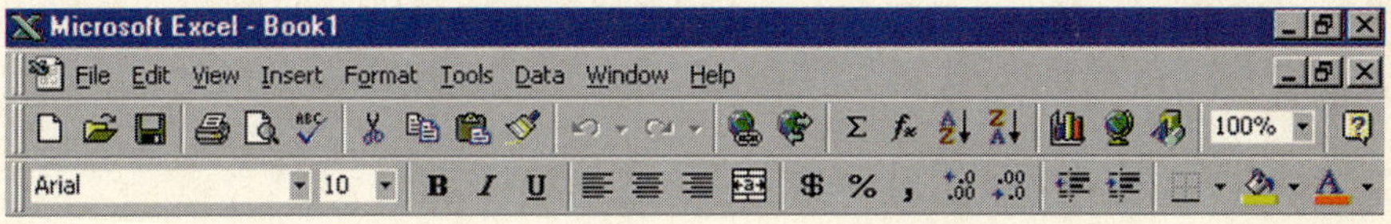

Figure 2.18
The Standard and Formatting toolbars for Excel.

Using Toolbar Buttons

As you are entering text, you can use toolbar buttons to turn features on or off at the location of the insertion point. The **insertion point** is the vertical bar that moves as you enter characters, use arrow commands to move around a document, or click the mouse.

Figure 2.19
The Standard and Formatting toolbars for PowerPoint with the bold, italic, and centering buttons pressed in, indicating that these features are turned on.

When you want a command to affect new text that you enter, click the desired toolbar button and then enter the text. The toolbar button appears as though it has been pressed in (Figure 2.19), which serves as a visual cue that that feature is on. When you want to turn off that feature, click the same toolbar button again. The button returns to its off condition.

You can also execute a toolbar command to affect previously entered text. First select the text to be changed by using a click and drag operation. The selected text appears with a black background. Click the desired toolbar button, and that command is executed for the selected text. Click anywhere in the document to turn off the selection. Such an operation affects only the selected text.

Figure 2.20
The Standard toolbar for Access.

File Task Buttons

The **file task buttons** include the New, Open, and Save buttons. You used the commands executed by these buttons in Session 1 of this module when you performed document manipulation tasks.

Printing and Spelling Buttons

The printing and spelling buttons control operations involved in printing and spell-checking a document.

Print

The Print button uses the current print settings and sends the specified document directly to the printer.

Print Preview

The Print Preview button invokes the Preview Window to show you how the document will appear when it is printed. For more information on this feature, refer to Session 1 of this module.

Spelling

Typically you will depend on Office's AutoCorrect feature to correct spelling errors as you create a document. If you insert text from some other document or import data from a spreadsheet, you may need to check the spelling as a separate task. To start the spell-checking process, you click the Spelling button. When the spelling checker finds what it thinks is a misspelled word, the Spelling and Grammar dialog box shown in Figure 2.21 appears. The spelling checker continues to check the entire document. You can check the spelling of a portion of a document by selecting that portion and then clicking the Spelling button.

A misspelled word appears in the Not in Dictionary box. You can enter the correct spelling, or you can click one of the replacements offered in the Suggestions box. When you click the Change button, the misspelled word is corrected. To correct all instances of that misspelling, click Change All. You can click Ignore to tell the spelling checker to skip a word that is not really misspelled but does not appear in the spelling checker's dictionary, such as technical terms, proper nouns, or acronyms. Click Ignore All to tell the spelling checker to skip all instances of that word in the document.

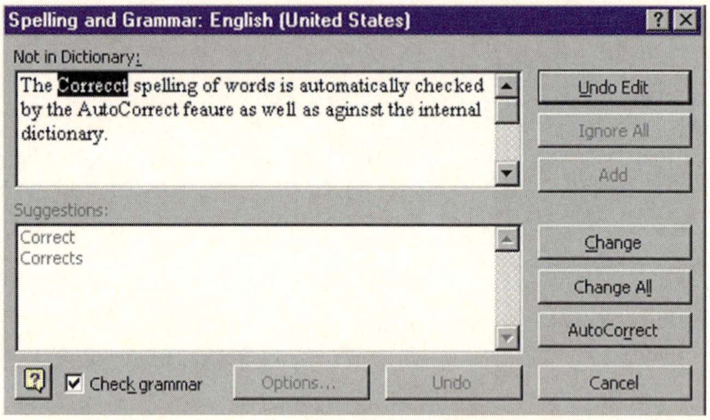

Figure 2.21
Word's Spelling and Grammar dialog box, where you can indicate how the spelling checker should correct errors it finds in your document.

Text Attribute Buttons

The **text attribute buttons** are used to boldface, italicize, and underline text. They can be used to turn an attribute on and then off when entering text or to change an attribute of selected text.

Bold

The Bold button is used to boldface text within a document. Boldfaced text appears darker than surrounding text.

TIMELY TIP

You can use the following keyboard shortcut commands instead of clicking toolbar buttons:

Bold	CTRL + **B**
Italic	CTRL + **I**
Underline	CTRL + **U**

Italics
The Italics button is used to italicize text within a document.

Underline
The Underline button is used to underscore text within a document.

Font Control Buttons

The **font control buttons** allow you to determine the font to use in the document or selection. A **font,** also called a typeface, is a specific style of type. Examples of different fonts include Times Roman, Helvetica, Letter Gothic, Elite, and Courier. Office applications give you several typeface styles to choose from.

Office applications use TrueType fonts. Microsoft automatically includes this set of fonts for use with any Windows application. Office applications can handle such fonts no matter what type of printer you use. This makes document generation much more reliable because Office does not have to use a less desirable font in place of the one you wanted. Different Office applications use a different default font. Word uses 12-point Times Roman. Excel uses 10-point Arial.

Font
The Font down arrow button displays a pull-down list box of available fonts (Figure 2.22). When you click the font of your choice, make certain that you first position the cursor where you want the new font to start or that you first select the text to which you want the new font applied.

Figure 2.22
The Font list box displaying the available fonts.

Font Size
Clicking the Font Size button displays a list box in which you can specify the size of the characters of a given font (Figure 2.23). The size of type is measured in **points.** The more points in a character, the larger that character will be when it prints. For example, 12-point type is larger than 10-point type. An inch consists of 72 points.

When you select a new font size, Word automatically keeps track of the new line height, character size, and spacing. It adjusts all spacing increments accordingly from this point on in the document (or for the selected text). Thus, once you have set your margins, you don't have to worry about them, even when you are printing larger characters. Page size is also automatically tracked, so page breaks occur at the correct locations.

Figure 2.23
Some of the font sizes available in Word.

Copy, Cut and Paste Buttons

The Copy, Cut, and Paste commands all use the Windows clipboard discussed in Session 1 of Module 1: Windows 95. The text included in a selected block is cut or copied from the document to the clipboard. You can then paste it elsewhere in the active document or in another document. Each time you issue a Cut or Copy command, any previous text or graphics on the clipboard is deleted and replaced with the newly selected text.

Copy
Clicking the Copy button leaves the original text in your document and copies it to the clipboard, replacing the previous contents of the clipboard.

Cut

Clicking the Cut button removes the selected text from your document and places it on the clipboard, replacing the existing contents of the clipboard.

Paste

Clicking the Paste button inserts cut or copied text anywhere in the document. First position the insertion point at the exact location to receive the cut or copied text, and then click the Paste button. The text is inserted, beginning at the location of the insertion point.

TIMELY TIP

The following keyboard shortcut commands can be used instead of clicking toolbar buttons:

Copy	CTRL + **C**
Cut	CTRL + **X**
Paste	CTRL + **V**

Hands-On Exercise: Copying, Cutting, and Pasting Text

This exercise demonstrates the Copy, Cut, and Paste commands using the 3Ch2 Cut and Paste Exercise document. In this exercise, you perform these commands from the toolbar.

1. **If necessary, start Word. Open the 3Ch2 Cut and Paste Exercise document.** (You may have to reset the directory using the Open dialog box.)

Click to open the Open dialog box.

Ch2 Cut and Paste Exercise Double-click to open the file. You should now see a document like that shown in Figure 2.24.

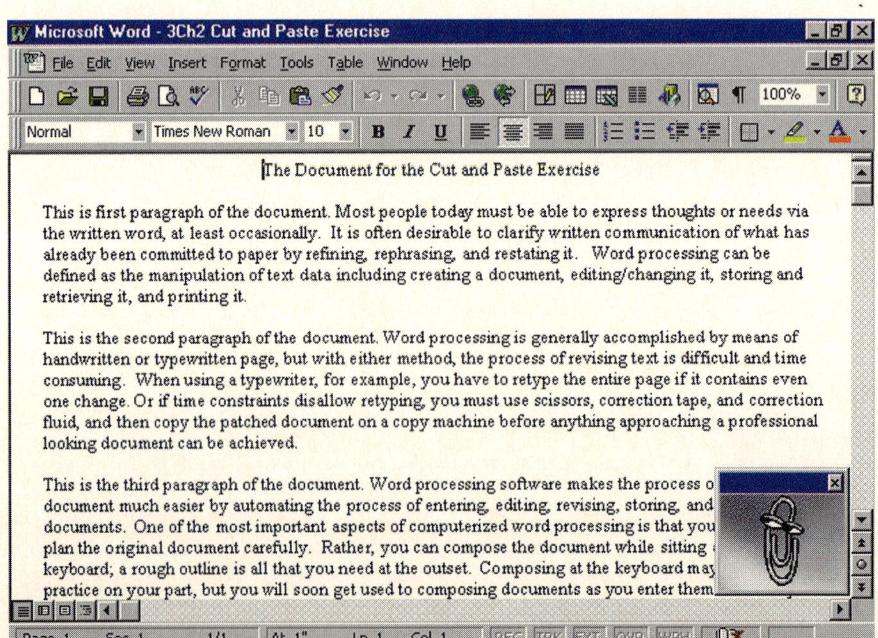

The Document for the Cut and Paste Exercise

This is first paragraph of the document. Most people today must be able to express thoughts or needs via the written word, at least occasionally. It is often desirable to clarify written communication of what has already been committed to paper by refining, rephrasing, and restating it. Word processing can be defined as the manipulation of text data including creating a document, editing/changing it, storing and retrieving it, and printing it.

This is the second paragraph of the document. Word processing is generally accomplished by means of handwritten or typewritten page, but with either method, the process of revising text is difficult and time consuming. When using a typewriter, for example, you have to retype the entire page if it contains even one change. Or if time constraints disallow retyping, you must use scissors, correction tape, and correction fluid, and then copy the patched document on a copy machine before anything approaching a professional looking document can be achieved.

This is the third paragraph of the document. Word processing software makes the process o document much easier by automating the process of entering, editing, revising, storing, and documents. One of the most important aspects of computerized word processing is that you plan the original document carefully. Rather, you can compose the document while sitting keyboard; a rough outline is all that you need at the outset. Composing at the keyboard ma practice on your part, but you will soon get used to composing documents as you enter them.

Figure 2.24
The 3Ch2 Cut and Paste Exercise document accessed by Word.

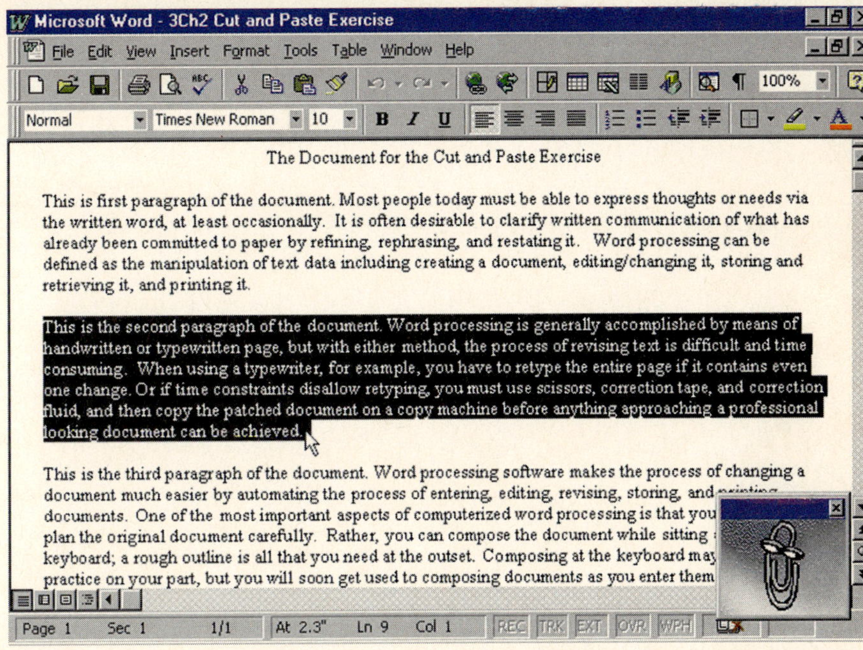

Figure 2.25
The selected text of the 3Ch2 Cut and Paste Exercise document.

2. Move to the beginning of the second paragraph, and select the text.

Click and drag — Click at the beginning of the left margin, to the left of *This is the second.* Drag to the end of the paragraph to extend the selection (Figure 2.25).

3. Issue the Copy command, and move to the end of the document.

 Click to copy the selected text to the clipboard.

CTRL + END — Press this key combination to go to the end of the document.

4. Insert a blank line and place the text at this location.

ENTER — Press to insert a blank line.

 Click to insert the text. You now have two copies of this paragraph in your document (Figure 2.26).

ENTER — Press to insert a blank line.

5. Cut the first paragraph and move it to the end of the document.

CTRL + HOME — Press to move to the beginning of the document (you can see that the second paragraph is still present).

Click and drag — Select the first paragraph (Figure 2.27).

 Click to delete the selected text from the document.

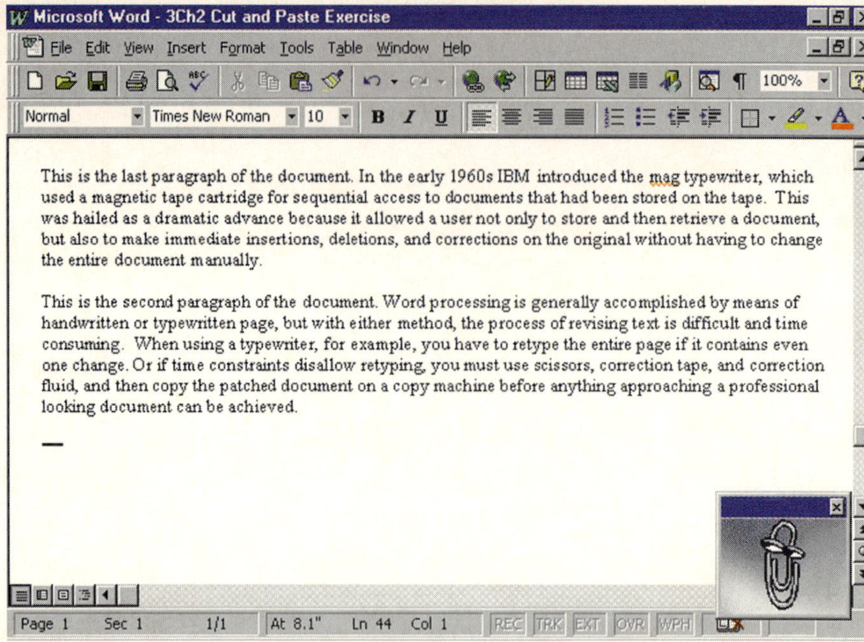

Figure 2.26
The text moved to its new location in the document.

6. **Insert the text at the end of the document.**

(CTRL) + (END) Press to go to the end of the document.

Click to paste the text. Your document should now look like Figure 2.28.

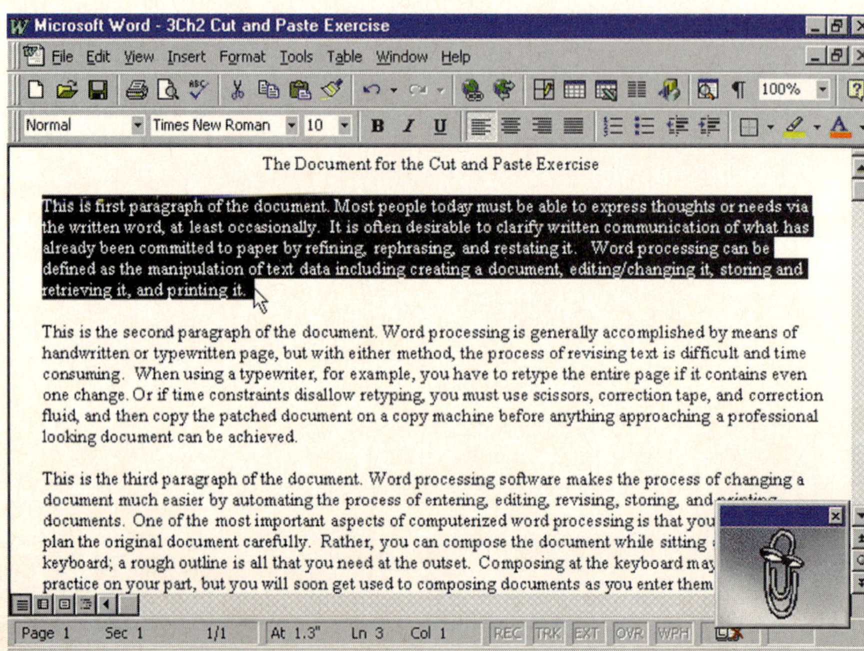

Figure 2.27
The document with the first paragraph selected.

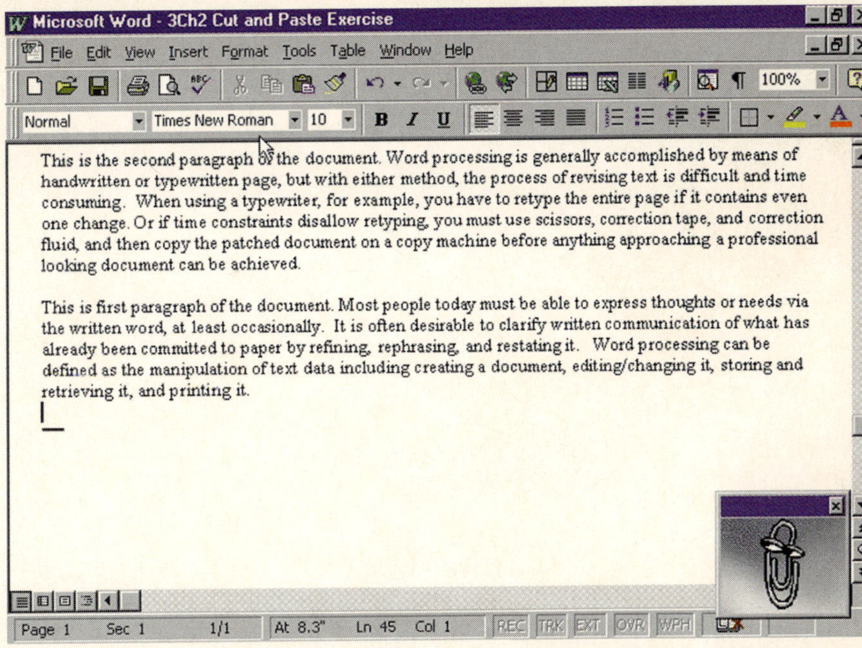

Figure 2.28
The document with the first paragraph moved to the end of the document.

7. **Clear the screen without saving the file.**

Click the document window Close button (on the menu bar). A prompt appears about saving the changes to the file.

Click so that the file is not saved.

TIMELY TIP

You can shorten the cut process by using a select and drag operation. First select the text; then position the mouse anywhere within the selected text and click and drag the text to the desired location. Once the drag operation begins, the mouse pointer includes a box with a thick-line border. Drag the mouse pointer to the desired location, and then release the left mouse button.

Reinforcing the Exercise

1. The Cut and Copy buttons copy selected parts of a document to the clipboard.
2. The Paste button copies information from the clipboard to the location of the insertion point in the document.
3. Each subsequent Cut or Paste command erases the prior contents of the clipboard and replaces it with the new selection.

Undo and Redo Buttons

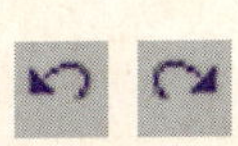

The Undo and Redo buttons allow you to easily correct mistakes that you have made while manipulating a document.

On Your Own

Repeat the Cut and Paste exercise that you just completed, using the shortcut commands given in the previous Timely Tip box.

Undo

By clicking the arrow portion of the Undo button, you can reverse a command that you just issued.

When you click the down arrow portion of the Undo button, a list of the tasks you just completed is displayed (Figure 2.29). Of course, what actions are listed depends on what you have just been doing. You can click any of these items to undo that action.

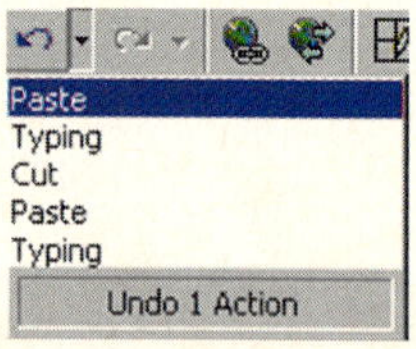

Figure 2.29
The Undo menu, which allows you to reverse tasks you have just performed.

Redo

The Redo button reexecutes the last command, if the command can be re-executed.

Alignment Buttons 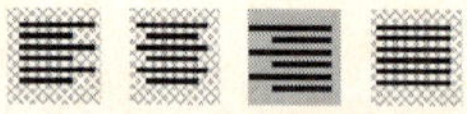

The alignment buttons allow you to control how text appears relative to the left and right margins of a column or page.

Align Left

The Align Left button is the default for Office applications. When you click Align Left, subsequent or selected text aligns along the left margin, and the right margin is ragged.

Center

The Center button moves the cursor to the middle of the line or column and centers any text you enter between the right and left margins. To deactivate center alignment and go to the next line, press (ENTER) and then click another alignment button.

To center text that you have already entered, select the text and click the Center button.

Align Right

The Align Right button allows you to right-justify text, with text aligned along the right margin and the left margin ragged. This option is used with dates, headings, and other data. When you enter the Align Right command, the cursor moves to the right margin. Type the text and then press (ENTER). To change the text alignment back, you then need to click the Align Left button.

If you forget to issue the Align Right command before you enter text, you can select that text and then click the Align Right button.

Justify

The Justify button results in even right and left margins, like those you see in magazines and newspapers. This is accomplished by adding space between characters and words so that the text margins are smooth.

Hands-On Exercise: Applying Text Attributes, Fonts, and Alignment

Juan and Isabel have made arrangements to rent the Civic Arena to a group of ferret fanciers. The president of the organization has come to the office to take advantage of one of the facility's advertised services: brochure preparation for a paid event. The president has a text file with the basic information that he wants the brochure to contain. He and Isabel now want to make the brochure more visually effective.

This exercise requires you to have Word started.

1. **Load the document 3Ch2 Ferret Expo Brochure.** The screen should look like Figure 2.30.

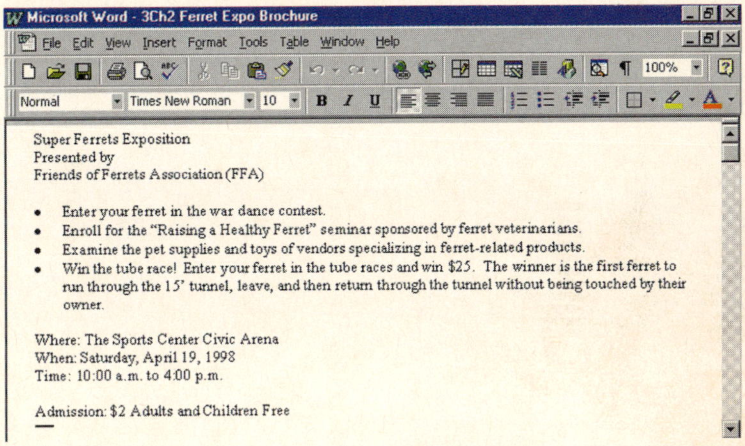

Figure 2.30
The 3Ch2 Ferret Expo Brochure document.

2. **Boldface and center the first three lines of the brochure.**

Click and drag — Select the first three lines of the document (Figure 2.31).

Click to make the lines appear in bold print.

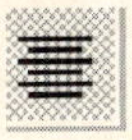

Click to make the lines appear centered. Your document should look like that shown in Figure 2.32.

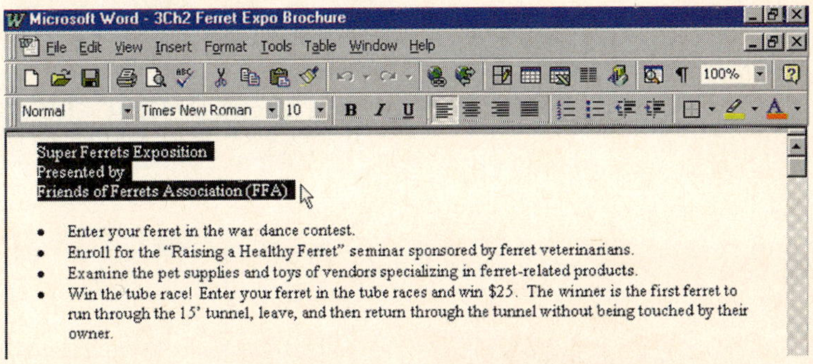

Figure 2.31
The first three lines of the brochure selected.

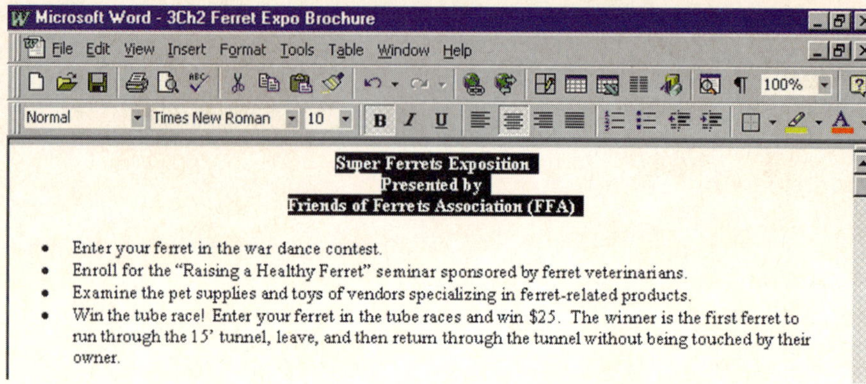

Figure 2.32
The boldfaced and centered lines of the brochure.

3. Change the font size of the first line to 36 point.

Click and drag — Select the first line.

 Click the down arrow of the Font Size list box to display the font size selections (Figure 2.33).

36 — Set the point size to 36. You will have to move down the list box using the scroll bar to see this option. Your document should now look like Figure 2.34.

4. Change the font size of the second line to 14 point.

Click and drag — Select the second line.

 Click the down arrow of the Font Size list box to display the font size selections.

14 — Set the point size to 14.

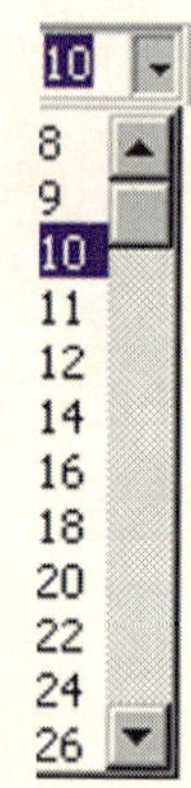

Figure 2.33
The Font Size list box ready for a choice to be made.

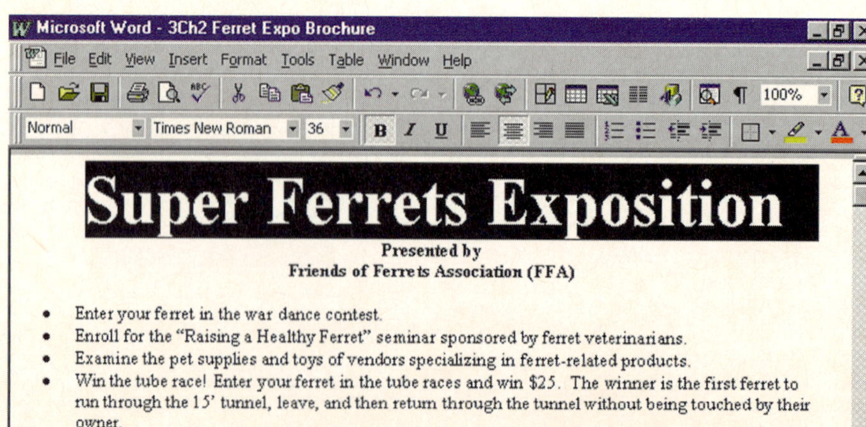

Figure 2.34
The first line with the new font size applied.

5. Change the font size of the third line to 20 point.

Click and drag   Select the third line.

   Click the down arrow of the Font Size list box to display the font size selections.

20   Set the point size to 20.

Click   Click anywhere to cancel the selection. Your document should now look like Figure 2.35.

6. Add blank lines before and after the second title line.

Click   Click at the beginning of the second line.

(ENTER)   Press to create a blank line before the second title line.

(END)   Click to go to the end of the line.

(ENTER)   Press to create a blank line after the second title line.

7. Add three blank lines after the third line.

(↓)   Press the down arrow key to move to the third title line.

(END)   Press to go to the end of the line.

(ENTER)   Press this key three times to create three blank lines. Your brochure should now look like Figure 2.36.

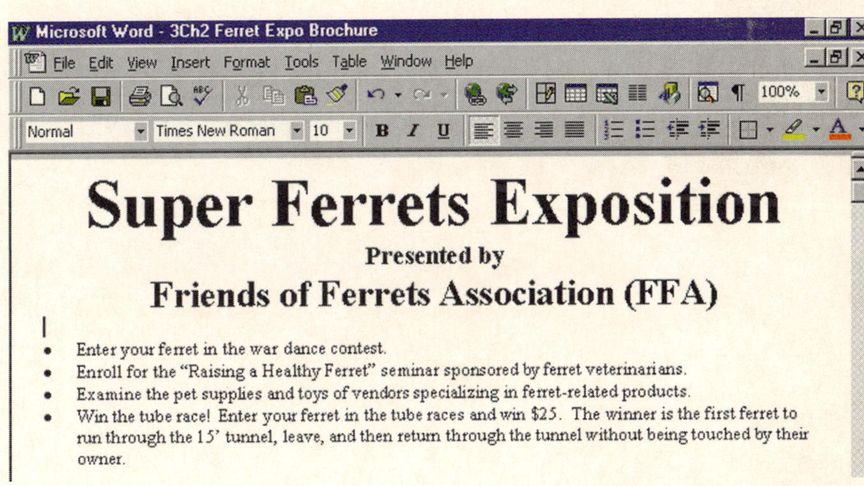

Figure 2.35
The brochure with the second and third lines changed.

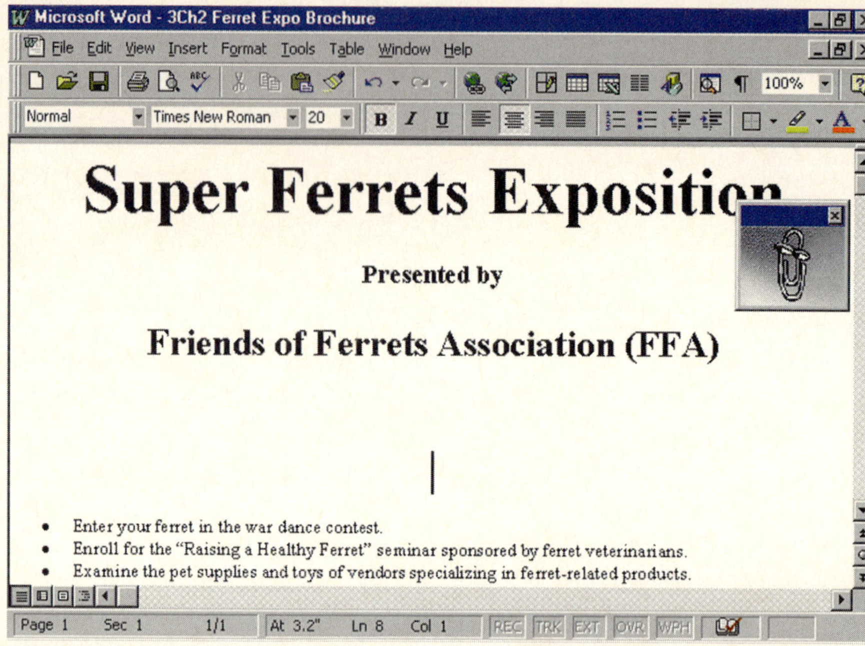

Figure 2.36
The brochure with the completed title lines.

8. **Change the font size of the bulleted text to 14 point.** Use the scroll bar to position the text so that you can see all of the bulleted text on the screen (Figure 2.37).

Click and drag — Select all six lines of the list.

Click the down arrow of the Font Size list box to display the font size selections.

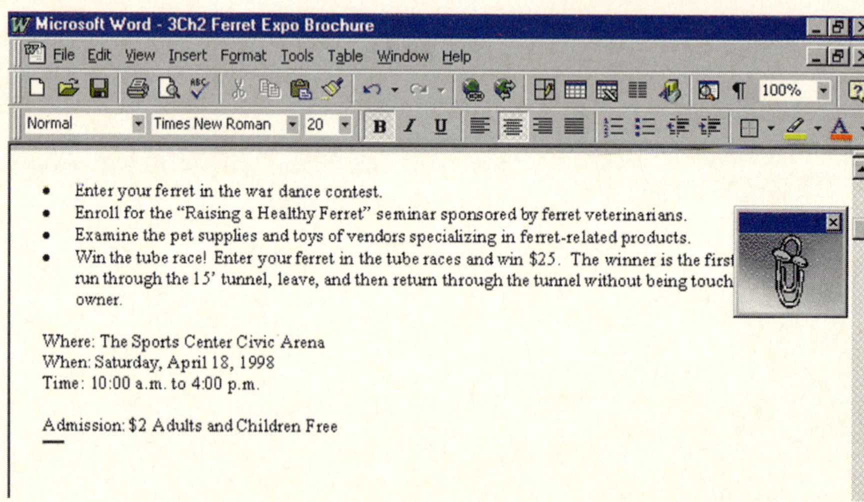

Figure 2.37
The document positioned for the next set of commands to be applied.

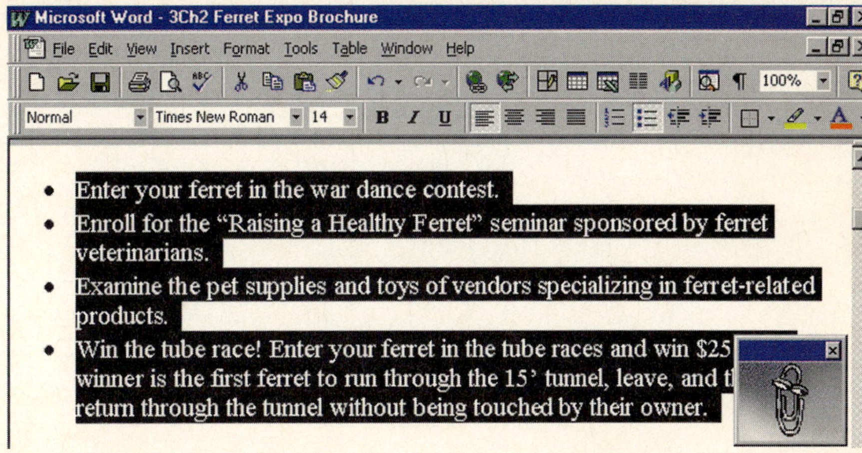

Figure 2.38
The bulleted list in a new font size.

14	Set the point size to 14. Your document should now look like Figure 2.38.

9. Move to the last line of bulleted text and insert three blank lines.

Click	Click to position the insertion point at the end of the last line of bulleted text.
(ENTER)	Press this key three times to insert three blank lines. Your brochure should now look like Figure 2.39.

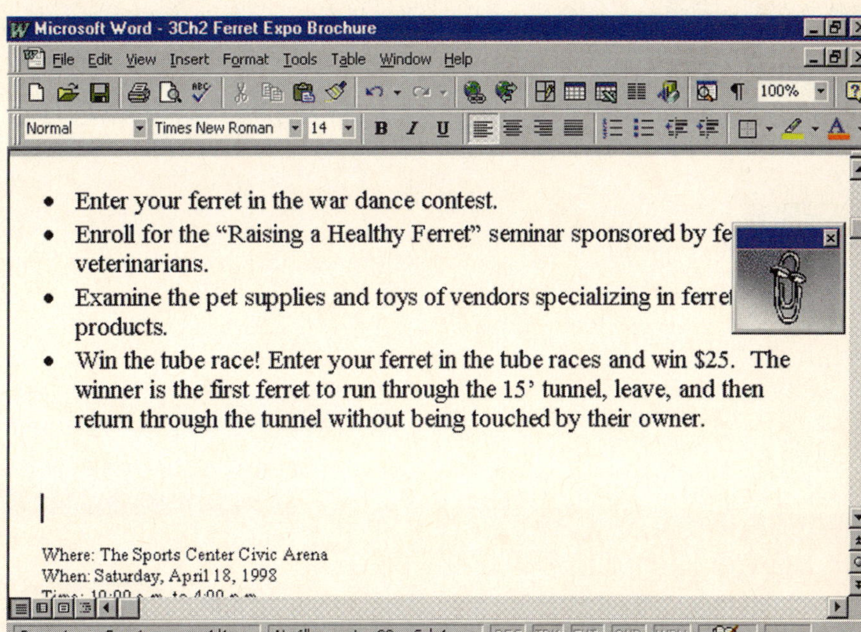

Figure 2.39
Three blank lines inserted at the end of the bulleted list.

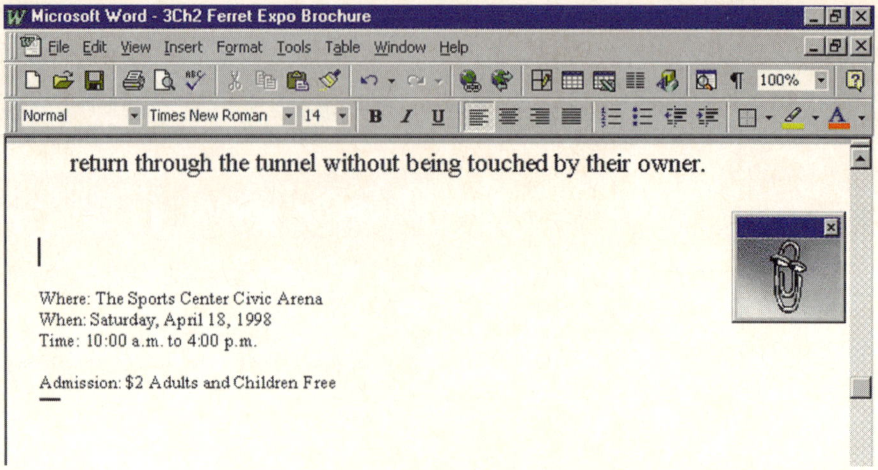

Figure 2.40
The document positioned for the next set of changes.

10. **Center and change the font size of the Where, When, and Time entries.** Use the scroll bar to display the rest of the document on the screen (Figure 2.40).

Click and drag — Select the Where, When, and Time lines.

 Click the down arrow of the Font Size list box to display the font size selections.

20 — Set the point size to 20.

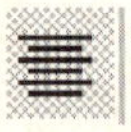 Click to center the three lines. Your brochure should now look like Figure 2.41.

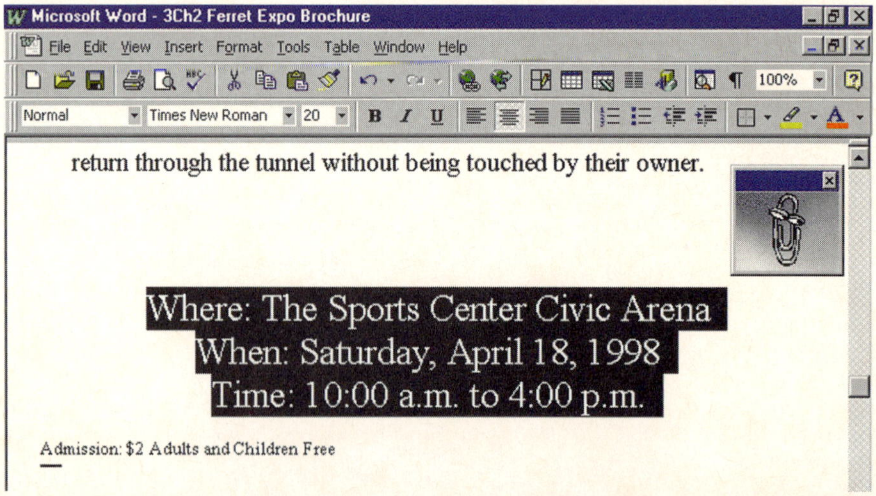

Figure 2.41
The Where, When, and Time lines centered with the font change.

11. Prepare the Admission line.

Click	Position the insertion point at the beginning of the line.
(ENTER)	Press this key six times to insert six blank lines.
Click and drag	Select the entire line.
	Click the down arrow of the Font Size list box to display the font size selections.
24	Set the point size to 24.
	Click to boldface the Admission line.
Click	Click anywhere to cancel the selection. Your brochure should now look like Figure 2.42.

12. Insert a border around the text.

Format	Click this item on the menu bar. The Border pull-down menu opens.
Borders and Shading . . .	Click to open the Borders and Shading dialog box.
Page Border	Click the Page Border tab. Your dialog box should now look like that shown in Figure 2.43.

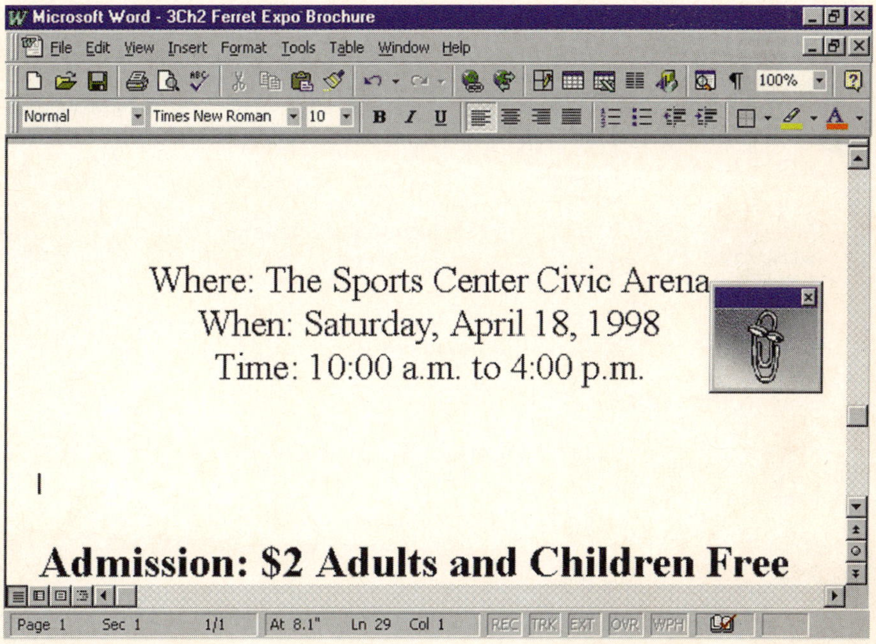

Figure 2.42
The Where, When, and Time lines of the brochure along with the Admission line.

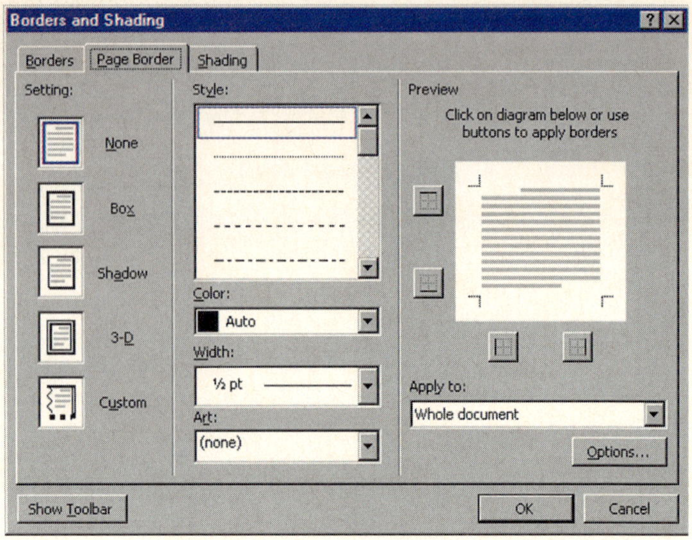

Figure 2.43
The Page Border tab of the Borders and Shading dialog box is used to place a border around a page.

Box — Click the Box option along the left side of the tab to create a box around the brochure.

Click to open the Border and Shading Options dialog box (Figure 2.44).

30 pt — Click the up arrow at the right end of each of the four boxes in the Margin section until this value appears.

Measure from: — Click on the down arrow at the right end Measure from: dialog box.

Text — Click on the Text option. The completed dialog box should look like Figure 2.45.

Click to close the Border and Shading Options dialog box.

Close the Border and Shading dialog box and return to the document.

12. Preview the brochure.

Click to open the Preview window.

Click to set Preview to One Page mode. The Preview window should look like Figure 2.46.

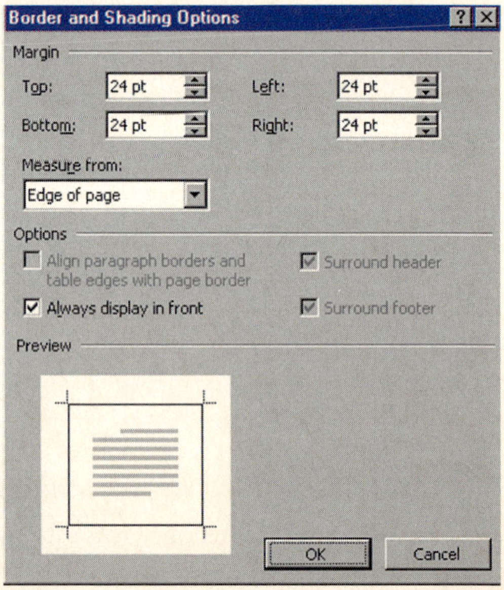

Figure 2.44
The Borders and Shading Options dialog box.

Close — Click to return to the document.

13. Record your name as the designer and print the brochure.

Click — Click at the end of the Admission line.

ENTER — Press this key twice to add two blank lines.

 Click the down arrow of the Font Size list box to display the font size selections.

8 — Set the point size to 8.

B — Click if necessary to turn off boldfacing.

 Click to set right justification.

Type: **By: *Your Name*** — Enter your name as the author of the brochure. The document should look similar to Figure 2.47.

 Click to send the brochure to the Print Manager for printing.

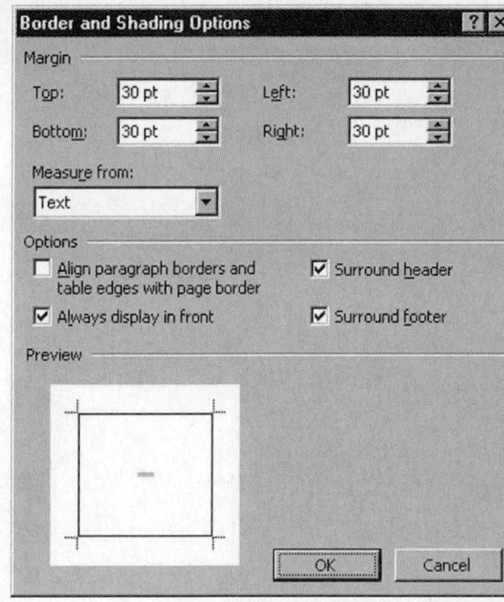

Figure 2.45
The completed Border and Shading Options dialog box.

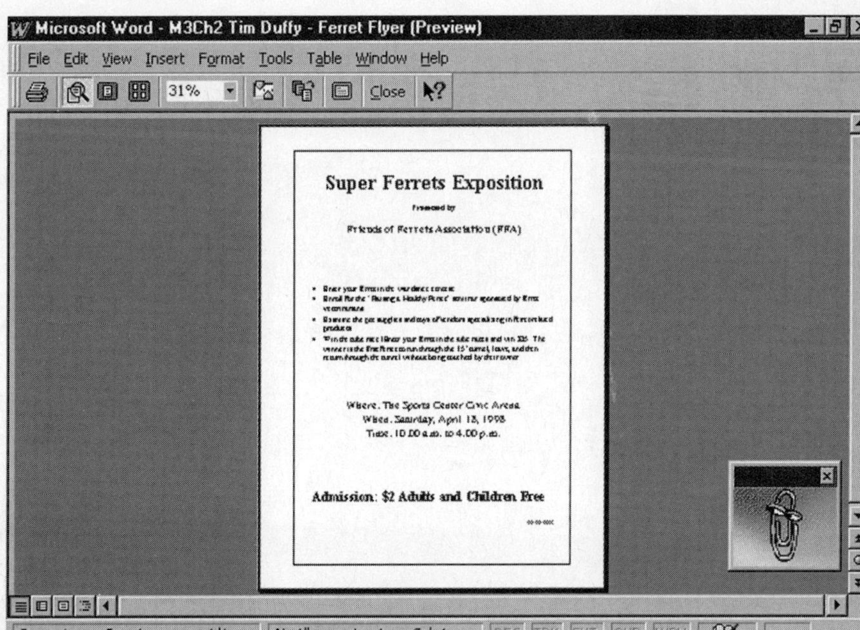

Figure 2.46
The brochure previewed in One Page mode.

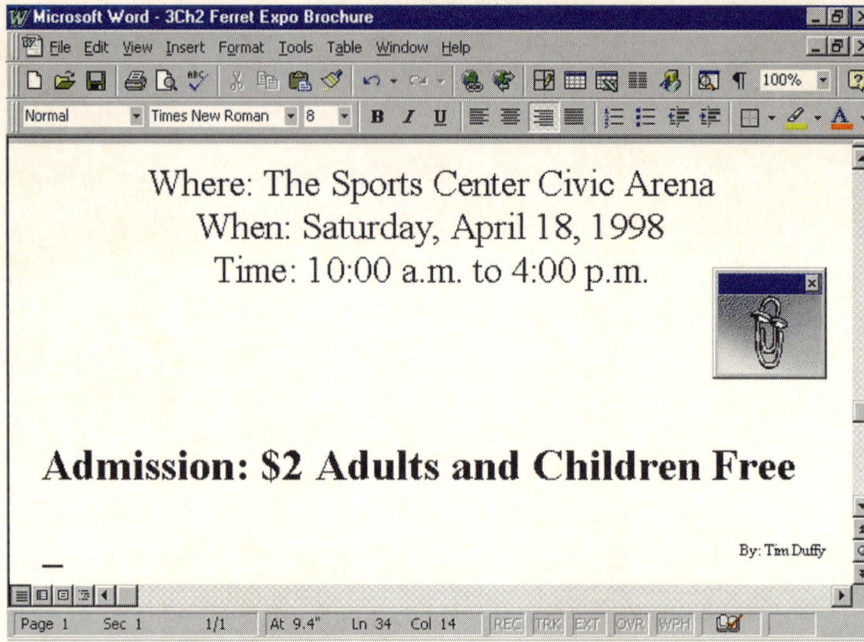

Figure 2.47
The author's name added to the document.

14. Save the brochure using your name.

File Click to open the File menu.

Save As . . . Click to open the Save As dialog box.

Type: **M3Ch2 *Your Name* Ferret Flyer** Enter your name as part of the document name.

Click to save the document.

15. Exit Word.

Click the Close button on the Word title bar.

Reinforcing the Exercise

1. When you select text in a document and then invoke a command, the command affects those selected lines.
2. Once you have selected text, you can perform various commands, such as changing the font, font size, and centering, on the text.
3. Changing such document attributes as font type, font size, boldfacing, and centering, can make the document look more interesting.

FORMAT PAINTER

The **Format Painter feature** allows you to apply all the attributes of selected text to another part of the document. First you select the text whose format you want to copy. Click the Format Painter button, and the pointer changes to a paint brush to indicate that the Format Painter feature is active. You then select the text to be affected. The paint brush pointer disappears, and the desired format is copied.

Hands-On Exercise: Using the Format Painter

This exercise requires you to have Excel started.

1. **Start Excel.** Open the 3Ch2 Format Painter Exercise document. You should now see a screen like that in Figure 2.48. Notice that the first column of text is larger than the other two columns. When you are finished with this exercise, all columns will appear the same.
2. **Examine the differences in the text.**

Week 1 Click this entry. Notice the font size is 14. Also note that the Bold and Italic buttons are pressed (Figure 2.49).

Week 2 Click this entry. Note the font size and the status of the Bold and Italic buttons (Figure 2.50).

3. **Apply the text attributes of the Week 1 column to the other columns.**

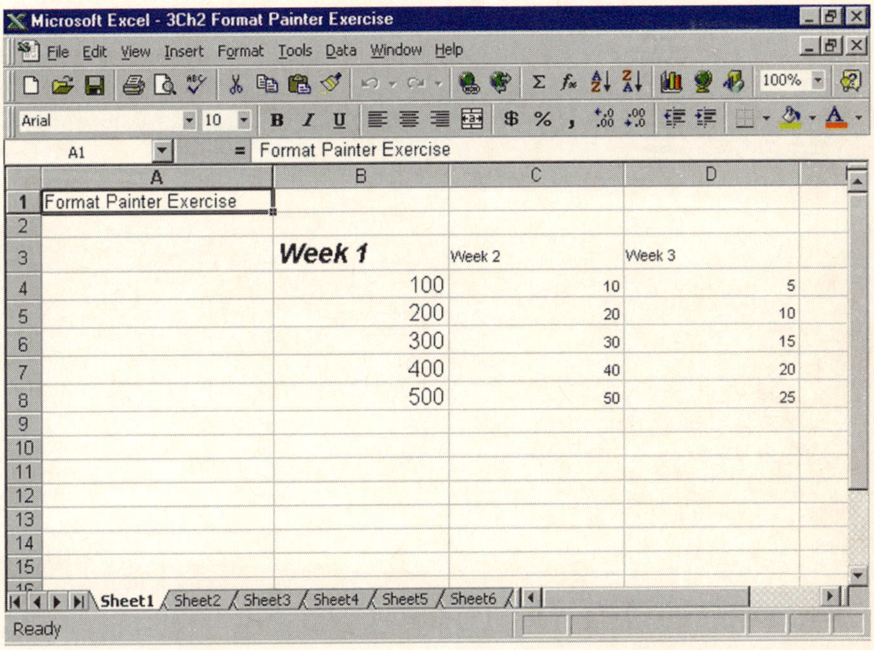

Figure 2.48
The 3Ch2 Format Painter Exercise document with columns containing different types of text.

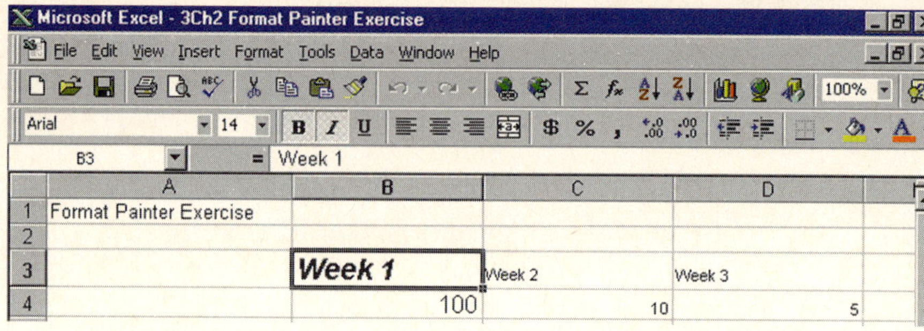

Figure 2.49
The toolbar attributes for the Week 1 cell.

Click and drag

Select the column beginning with *Week 1* and ending with *500.* Your screen should now look like Figure 2.51.

Click this button. The pointer changes to a large plus sign with a paint brush to the right.

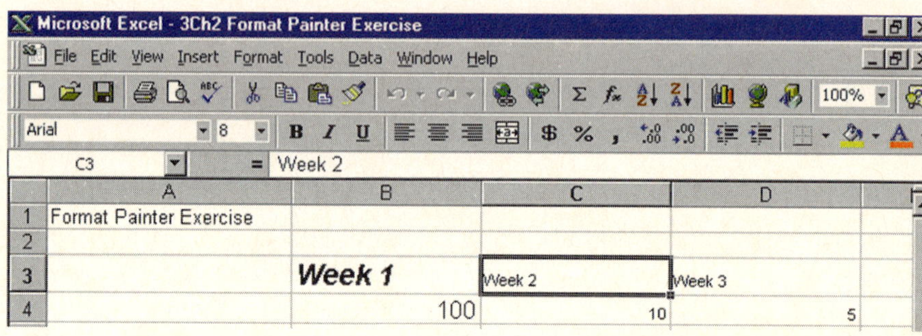

Figure 2.50
The toolbar attributes for the Week 2 cell.

Click and drag

Select the Week 2 and Week 3 columns. Release the mouse button, and the text changes as shown in Figure 2.52.

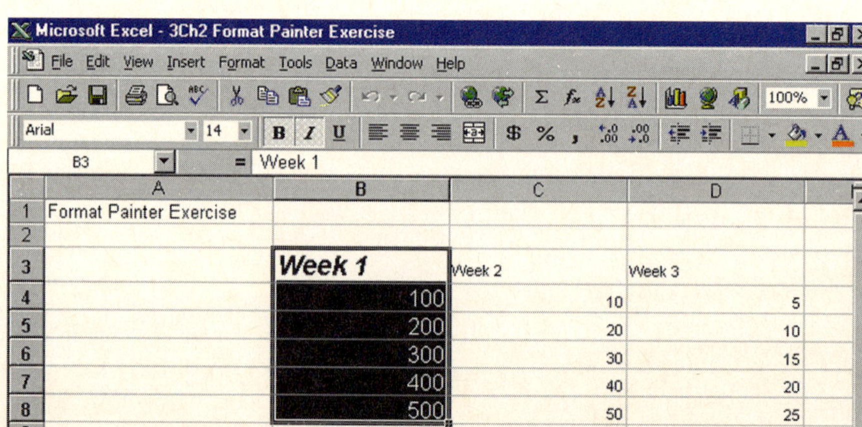

Figure 2.51
The selection from which the format is to be copied.

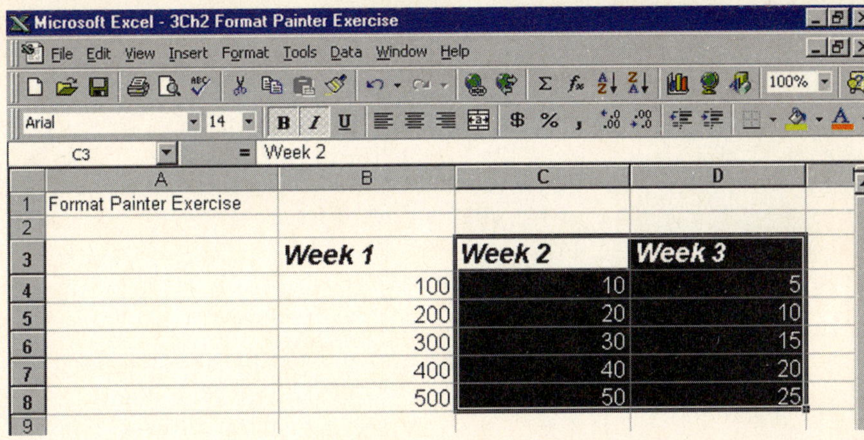

Figure 2.52
The selected area with the copied format applied.

4. **Reverse the action that you just took.**

Click so that the text appears as it did before the Format Painter command was issued.

Click to remake the format changes.

5. **Print the document.**

Click to send the document to the Print Manager.

6. **Exit Excel without saving the document.**

Click the Close button on the Excel title bar.

Click to decline saving the changes to the 3Ch2 Format Painter Exercise document.

Reinforcing the Exercise

1. You can use the Format Painter button to copy the text attributes of one selection to another.
2. When you are in Format Painter mode, the mouse pointer changes to a paint brush.
3. You can reverse the text attributes changed by the Format Painter by clicking the Undo button.

OFFICE ART CAPABILITIES

All Microsoft Office applications have a drawing capability called the **Office Art feature** that allows you to draw lines, arrows, shapes, shadows, and 3-D images and add them to existing documents.

Figure 2.53
The Drawing toolbar typically appears at the bottom of the screen.

This feature is accessed by issuing the View, Toolbars command sequence and then selecting the **Drawing toolbar.** The toolbar appears at the bottom of the screen (Figure 2.53). Each of the buttons on the Drawing toolbar are discussed in Table 2.3.

Table 2.3 Drawing Toolbar Buttons

Button	Name	Function
Draw	Draw	Provides a menu to control such things as rotating, aligning, and nudging of graphic items as well as changing the shape of an inserted graphic.
	Select Objects	Can be used in a drag operation to include those graphic items in a selection before additional commands are entered.
	Free Rotate	Allows you to grab a colored dot handle of a selected image and rotate that image in the document.
AutoShapes	AutoShapes	Displays menus from which you can select an image to insert.
	Line	Allows you to draw a line in a document by using a click and drag operation to indicate its beginning and ending points.
	Arrow	Allows you to draw an arrow in a document by using a click and drag operation to indicate its beginning and ending points.
	Rectangle	Allows you to draw a rectangle in a document by using a click and drag operation to two diagonal points.
	Oval	Allows you to draw an oval in a document by using a click and drag operation.
	Text Box	Allows you to create a box in which text can be added.
	Insert Word Art	Displays a menu from which you can select the type of text art that you want to include in your document.
	Fill Color	The down arrow displays a palette from which you can select a color to fill a selected image. Click the other part of the button to fill the image with the indicated color.
	Line Color	The down arrow displays a palette from which you can select a color for lines. Click the other part of the button to draw lines with the indicated color.
	Font Color	The down arrow displays a palette from which you can select a color for text. Click the other part of the button to change the text of a selection to the indicated color.
	Line Style	Allows you to select the type of line used to draw an image.
	Dash Style	Allows you to create different styles of dashed lines.
	Arrow Style	Allows you to select a type of arrow.
	Shadow	Allows you to select shadowing for an image.
	3-D	Allows you to determine how a 3-D image is to be displayed.

Hands-On Exercise: Using the Office Art Feature

This exercise requires you to have Word started.

1. **Open the 3Ch2 Your Name Ferret Flyer document that you created earlier in this session.**

2. **Position the insertion point.**

Click — Position the insertion point on the first blank line following the line with *FFA* in it.

3. **Activate the Drawing toolbar.**

View — Click to open the View pull-down menu.

Toolbars — Click to open the Toolbars pull-down menu.

Drawing — Click to display the Drawing toolbar. Your screen should now look like that shown in Figure 2.54.

4. **Insert a ribbon image in this blank area of the document.**

 — Click this button on the toolbar to left-justify the image.

AutoShapes — Click to activate the menu shown in Figure 2.55.

Stars and Banners — Click this option to see the menu displayed in Figure 2.56.

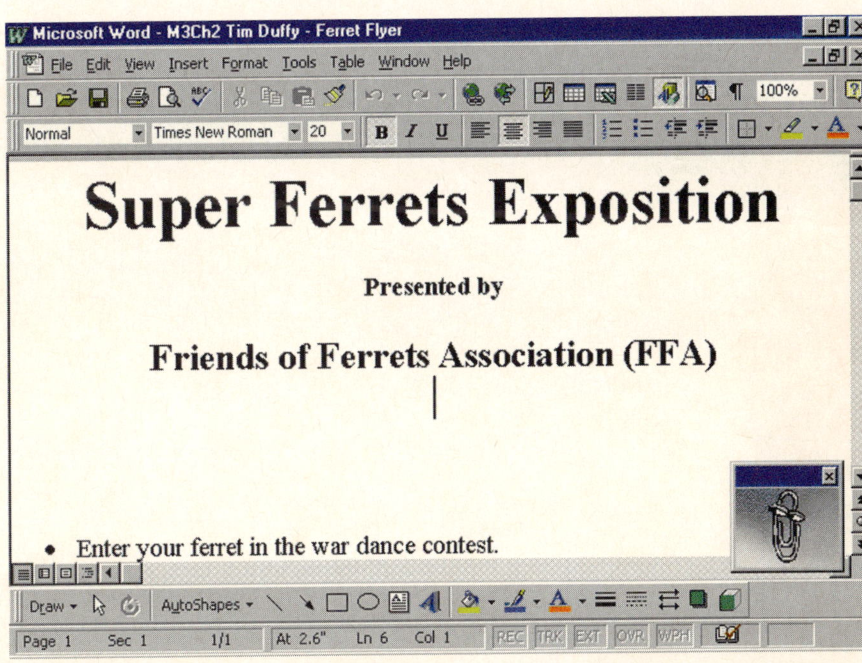

Figure 2.54
The ferret brochure with the Drawing toolbar displayed and insertion point repositioned, ready for an image to be inserted.

Curved Down Ribbon	Click this image to select this ribbon image. The mouse pointer turns into a cross-hair so that you can position the image in the document.
Click	Click the left portion of the line you just left-justified. The ribbon appears as shown in Figure 2.57. The squares around the selected image are called **drag handles.**

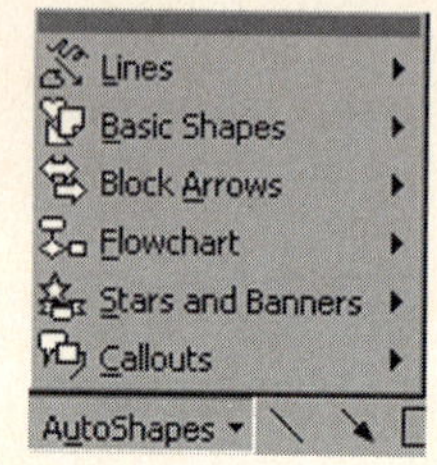

Figure 2.55
The AutoShapes menu offers various kinds of graphic images.

5. **Resize the ribbon image.**

Drag	Click the middle drag handle on the right side of the ribbon image (the pointer should now look like a double arrow) and drag it to the right of the document (to the position of the rightmost character). Your document should look like Figure 2.58.
Click	Click anywhere outside the image to deselect it.

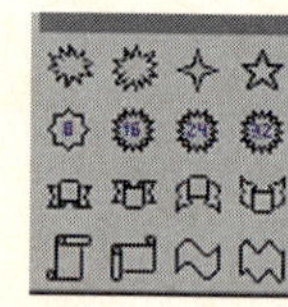

Figure 2.56
The different types of star and banner images that can be embedded in a document.

6. **Examine the document.**

Click to activate Print Preview and examine the revised document (Figure 2.59). Leave Print Preview when you are finished.

7. **Print the document.**

Click to send the document to the printer.

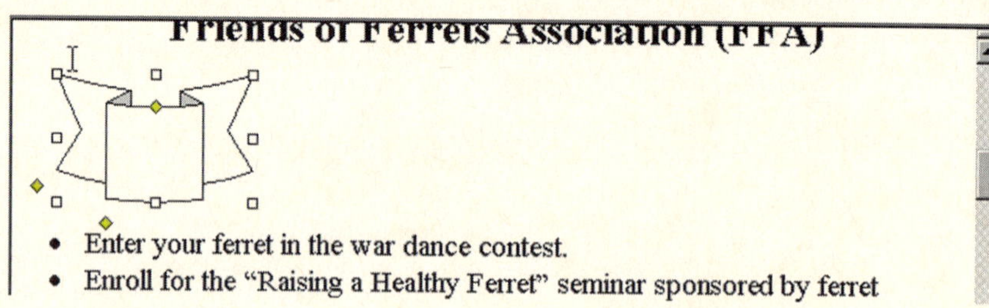

Figure 2.57
The ribbon image in the ferret document with the drag handles surrounding it.

8. **Save the document.**

Click to save the file.

9. **Close the document.**

Click the Close button on the menu bar.

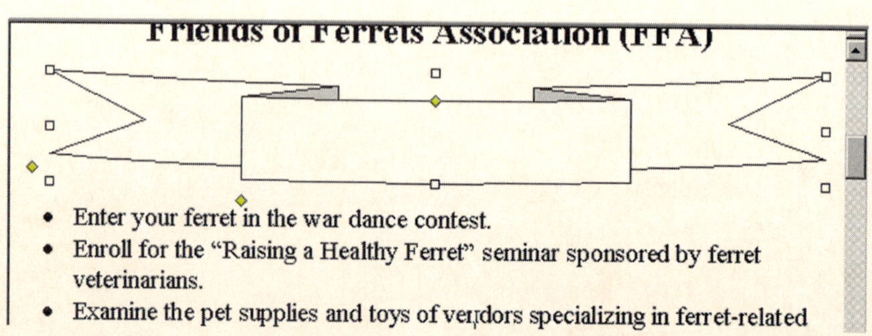

Figure 2.58
The document with the resized ribbon image.

Using the WordArt Feature 

Office provides another graphics feature called WordArt, which allows you to manipulate text to form a variety of eye-catching shapes. You can access WordArt from the Drawing toolbar. Once you have created a WordArt image, you can combine it with other shapes you have created and then insert them all into a document.

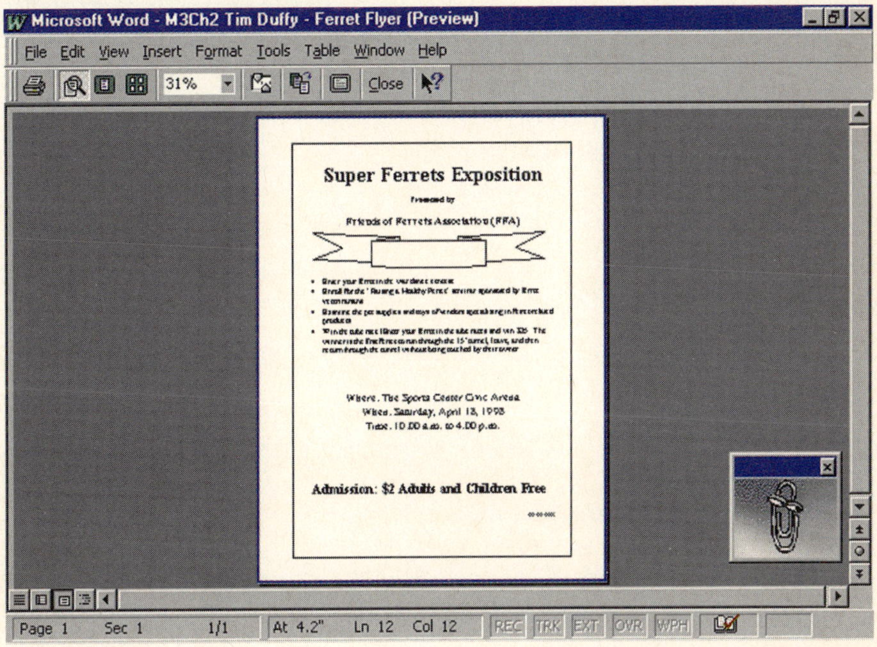

Figure 2.59
The document with the inserted image shown in Page Preview.

Hands-On Exercise: Using More Office Art Features

1. **Activate a new document.**

Click to open a blank document. Activate the Drawing toolbar if it is not displayed.

2. **Use the WordArt feature.**

Click this button on the Drawing toolbar to open the WordArt Gallery dialog box shown in Figure 2.60.

Double-click the shadowed text option. The Edit WordArt Text dialog box shown in Figure 2.61 appears.

Figure 2.60
The WordArt dialog box for selecting the type of word art to be inserted in an Office document.

Type: ***Your Name***

Click to insert a shadowed image of your name in the document.

Click — Click anywhere outside the image to turn off the selection. Your document should now look like Figure 2.62.

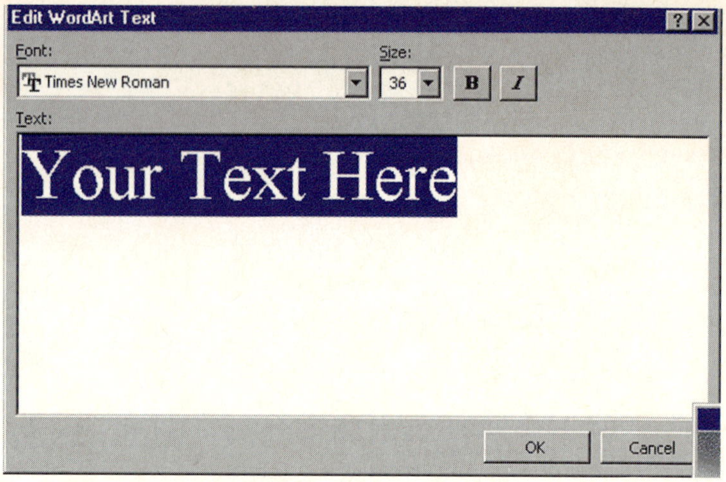

Figure 2.61
The dialog box for entering your WordArt text.

3. Move past the graphic.

(CTRL) + (END) — Use this shortcut command to move the end of the document.

(ENTER) — Press six times to insert blank lines in the document.

4. Draw an oval around your name.

Click this button on the drawing toolbar. The pointer now turns into a cross-hair.

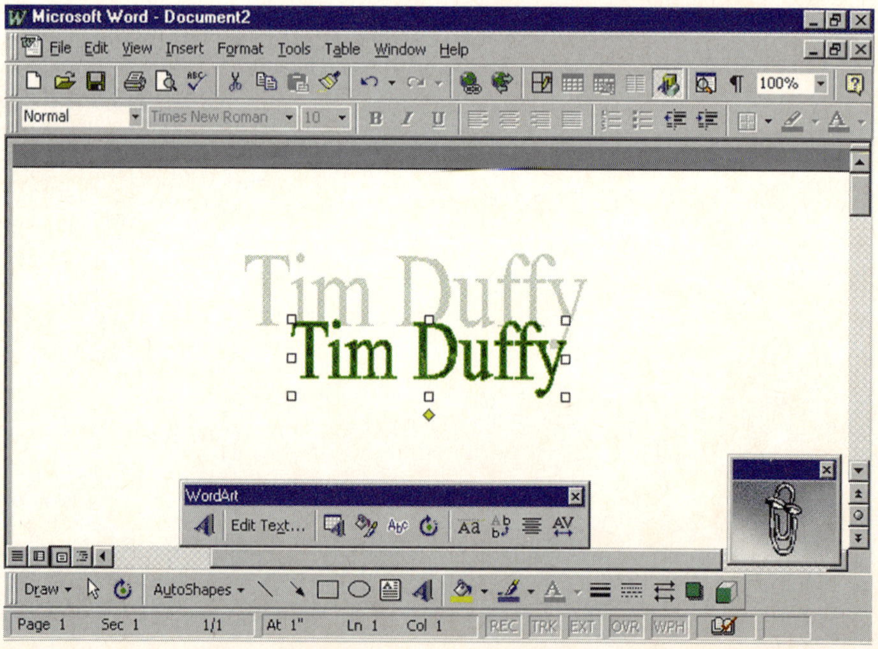

Figure 2.62
Shadowed image of author's name inserted in the document.

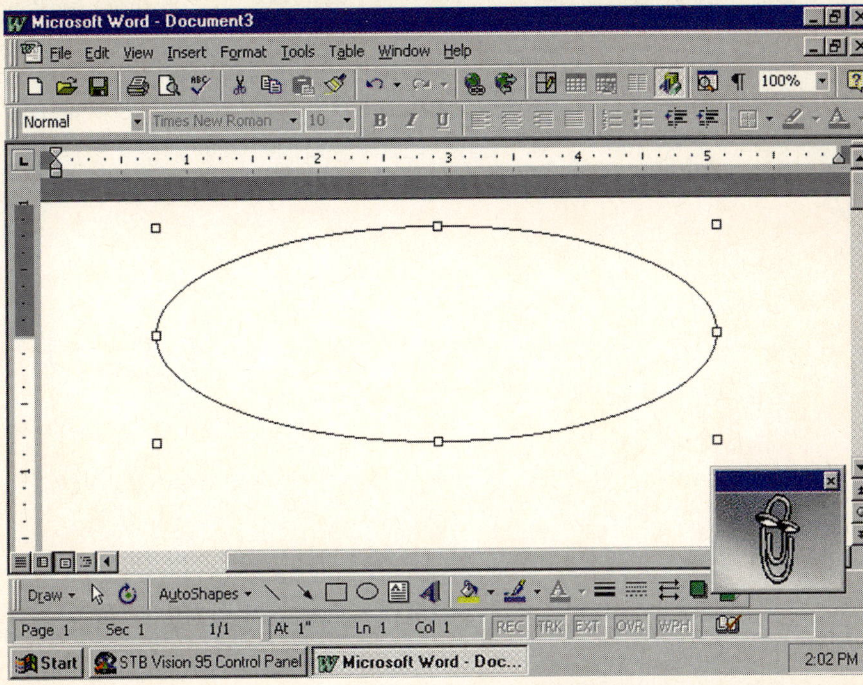

Figure 2.63
The oval has made your name disappear.

Drag — Position the cross-hair in the upper-left corner above your name. drag to center your name in the oval. When you release the mouse, your name disappears (Figure 2.63).

5. Make your name visible again.

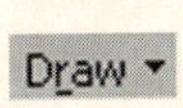

Click to open the Draw menu (Figure 2.64). This menu controls the display of objects you've drawn.

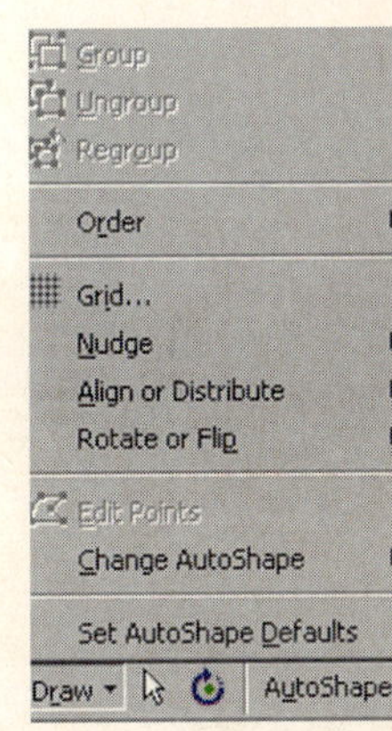

Figure 2.64
The Draw menu used to control how objects are displayed.

Order — Invoke the Order menu (Figure 2.65). You use this menu to determine which object is displayed first. Currently, the oval is displayed first so it obscures your name image.

Send to Back — Click this option to reverse the display: Your name image is displayed first and does not obscure the oval, which is displayed second (Figure 2.66).

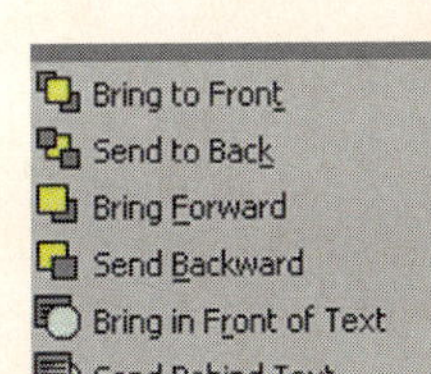

Figure 2.65
The Order menu controls which object is displayed first.

6. Color the oval light yellow.

Click the down arrow of the Fill Color button. A palette like that shown in Figure 2.67 appears.

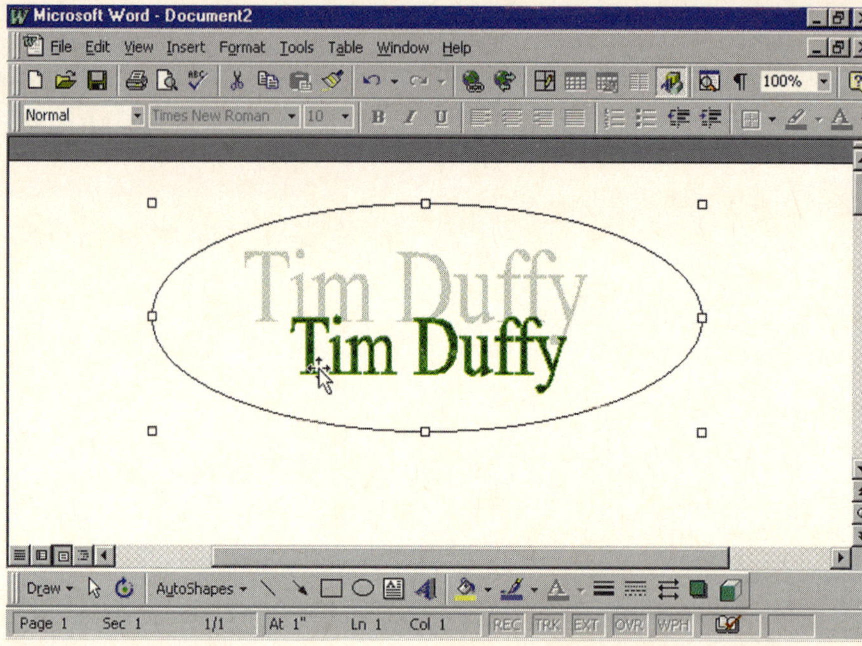

Figure 2.66
The document with your name image in the foreground.

Light Yellow	Click this color.
Click	Click anywhere in the document to turn off the selection. Your finished graphic should look like Figure 2.68.

7. **Save the document using the name M3Ch2 Draw Exercise.** You might like to use this for letterhead.
8. **Print the document.**
9. **Continue to use this document to experiment with any of the Draw commands that interest you.** Use the Save As command to save any document you create using a name of your choice.
10. **Close the document and exit Word.**

Figure 2.67
The color palette for the Fill Color button.

On Your Own

- Open the ferret brochure with the ribbon image that you just inserted.
- Add other images, as shown in Figure 2.69, as well as any images that you think should be included.
- Save the document as M3Ch2 On Your Own using the Save As command.

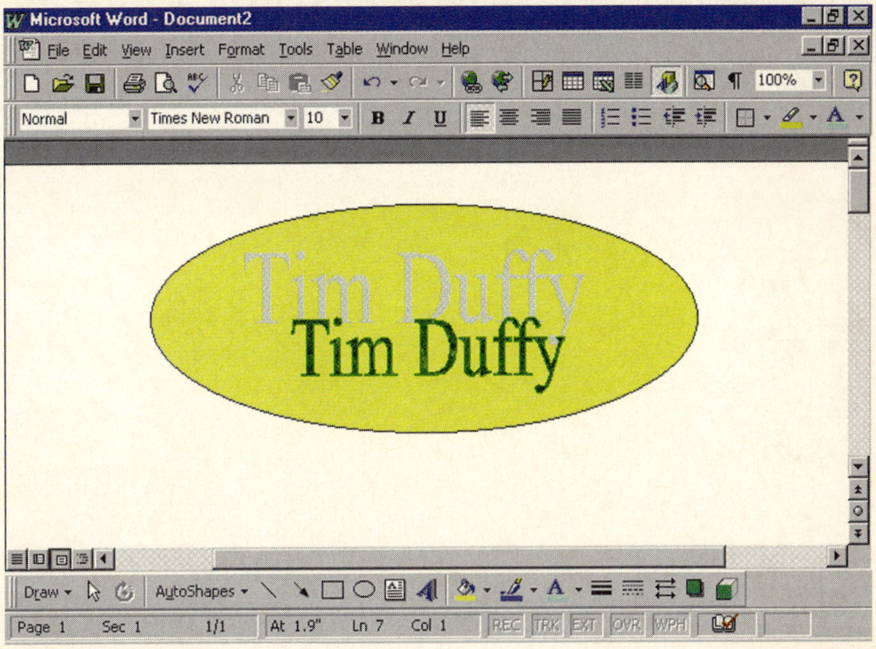

Figure 2.68
The finished graphic containing your name.

Reinforcing the Exercise

1. The Office Art feature of Office is available to all Office applications.
2. The Drawing toolbar is used to create and insert images in a document.
3. The Office Art feature of Office has a number of pre-drawn objects that can be embedded within a document.
4. When placing multiple objects at the same location in the document, you have to send one to the background to display the other.

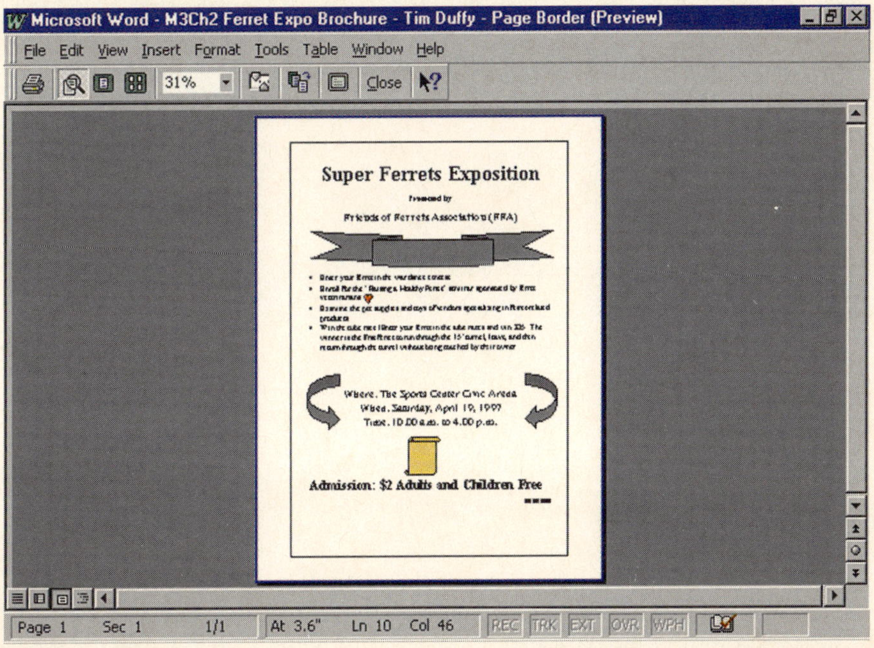

Figure 2.69
Graphic features added to the ferret brochure.

SESSION REVIEW

Office applications provide the same type of help as Windows. All Office applications provide help through the Help Topics dialog box, which contains the Contents, Index, and Find tabs. The Office Assistant is Office's primary vehicle for providing help to the user.

As an alternative to using the mouse, Office applications offer a number of keystroke commands that provide a consistent means of moving through documents. Arrow keys and PGUP and PGDN keys, sometimes combined with CTRL, provide a means of navigating around a document.

The process of editing, or changing, a document involves tasks such as inserting text, deleting text, or correcting spelling errors. You can insert text in either Insert or Overwrite mode. Office applications provide the AutoCorrect feature, which corrects spelling errors automatically as you type. In addition, Word marks misspelled words with a wavy red line and any grammar errors with a wavy green line.

Office applications make extensive use of toolbars. Toolbars provide a graphic means of entering commonly used commands: You click a button instead of entering commands through an application's menu structure. Commonly used toolbars include the Standard and Formatting toolbars. Several toolbars can be active for any Office application and can share common groupings of buttons, including file task buttons, printing and spelling buttons, text attribute buttons, font control buttons, the Cut and Paste buttons, the Undo and Redo buttons, and alignment buttons.

The Format Painter feature allows you to copy text attributes such as boldfacing, fonts, italics, and underlining from one part of a document and apply them to text in another part of the document.

Using a toolbar button often requires clicking a button to turn on a feature, entering text, and then clicking the button again to turn that feature off. A toolbar button command can also be applied to selected text within a document. Clicking certain toolbar buttons can open dialog boxes that require your interaction.

The Office Art feature is activated by activating the Drawing toolbar. It provides a number of images that can be inserted in a document. After inserting an image or shape in a document, you can resize it, apply color, change the line color, and make other adjustments.

KEY TERMS AND CONCEPTS

AutoCorrect feature 3–40
drag handles 3–71
Drawing toolbar 3–69
editing 3–39
file task buttons 3–49
font 3–50
font control buttons 3–50
Format Painter feature 3–65
Insert mode 3–41
insertion point 3–48
Office Art feature 3–68
Overwrite mode 3–41
point 3–50
text attribute buttons 3–49

SESSION QUIZ

Multiple Choice

1. Which of the following features is not supported in the Draw feature of Microsoft Office?
   a. changing the color of an embedded image
   b. changing the rotation aspect of a drawn image
   c. resizing an embedded image
   d. All of the above are supported.
2. Which of the following statements about the Office Art feature is false?
   a. Only predrawn images can be inserted in a document.
   b. Many drawing operations require a drag operation using the mouse.
   c. You cannot place two images at the same location because one image will be hidden.
   d. Before you can change an image, you must select it and the drag handles must be displayed.
3. Which of the following is not a way of correcting a spelling error in an Office application?
   a. The application uses the AutoCorrect feature to automatically correct a spelling error.
   b. Word indicates a misspelling with a wavy red line.
   c. You use the Format menu to start the spelling checker.
   d. All of the above are ways to correct spelling in an Office document.
4. Which of the following is a correct statement regarding the Cut and Paste commands?
   a. The Cut command results in two copies of the text remaining in the document.
   b. The Copy command never erases the contents of the clipboard.
   c. The Copy command can be invoked by clicking the Copy button or by pressing CTRL + C.
   d. The Paste command clears the contents of the clipboard.
5. Which of the following statement(s) about editing is/are correct?
   a. Overwrite mode pushes existing characters to the left.
   b. Insert mode pushes characters to the left.
   c. Pressing BKSP erases the character at the insertion point.
   d. Pressing DEL erases the character at the insertion point.

True/False

6. Toolbar buttons provide shortcuts for executing common Office commands.
7. The Insert WordArt button of the drawing toolbar allows you to send an image to the back to make another image visible.
8. The Cut and Copy buttons can both affect the clipboard.
9. The Format Painter takes the attributes and characteristics of one portion of text and allows you to apply them to other text.
10. Many commands found in toolbars can be used for entering text or applied to existing text.

SESSION REVIEW EXERCISES

1. Define or describe each of the following:
   a. Office Art feature
   b. toolbar
   c. Format Painter
   d. AutoCorrect
   e. alignment
2. The ______________ feature contains a number of preformed images that can be inserted in a document.
3. The ______________ arrow moves you up a line.
4. The ______________ + ______________ shortcut command moves you to the beginning of a document.
5. The ______________ key moves you down a screen.
6. The ______________ + ______________ shortcut command moves you to the end of a document.
7. The ______________ feature automatically corrects a spelling error for you.
8. Clicking the ______________ button opens a dialog box you can use to check the spelling of a document.
9. ______________ mode moves text to the right as you enter new text.
10. The ______________ key deletes the character at the insertion point.
11. When text in a Word document has a wavy green line under it, you can correct the grammar by ______________ -clicking the words to active a grammar context menu.
12. The ______________ button opens a dialog box for loading a document.
13. The ______________ button automatically sends a document to the Print Manager.
14. A/an ______________ is also called a typeface.
15. Both the Cut and Copy commands change the contents of the ______________.
16. The ______________ button leaves the original contents and copies the selected text to the clipboard.
17. The ______________ button allows you to reverse a command.
18. The ______________ button positions text equidistant between the right and left margins.
19. The ______________ button opens a blank document.
20. The ______________ menu can be used to open another document.
21. The Office Art feature many times requires you to perform a ______________ operation using a mouse to draw an image or shape.
22. You can resize an image by using one of the ______________ handles in conjunction with the mouse.
23. The ______________ feature allows you to make interesting images based on text that you enter.

24. Color ______________ are used to determine the fill or line color for an image.

25. Before an image can be changed, it must be ______________.

COMPUTER EXERCISES

1. Open the 3Ch2 Painter Exercise file from the data directory or disk (Figure 2.70). Notice that a number of special effects have been applied to the first line of the document. The other lines in the document appear in the default font and point size with none of those special effects.
   a. Use the Format Painter feature to apply the special characteristics of the first line to the other lines in the document.
   b. Center the remaining lines of the document.
   c. Place your name in the upper-left corner of the document using 8-point type.
   d. Print the document.
   e. Use the Save As command to save the document with the name M3Ch2 Exercise 1.
2. Clear the screen and open the 3Ch2 Text Attribute and Align file. Your document should look like Figure 2.71.
   a. Select each line of text with the mouse, and then perform each indicated task on the appropriate line. For example, the first line, *Center this text,* should be centered using the Center button.
   b. Place your name in the upper-left corner of the document.
   c. Save your work with the name M3Ch2 Exercise 2.
   d. Print the document.

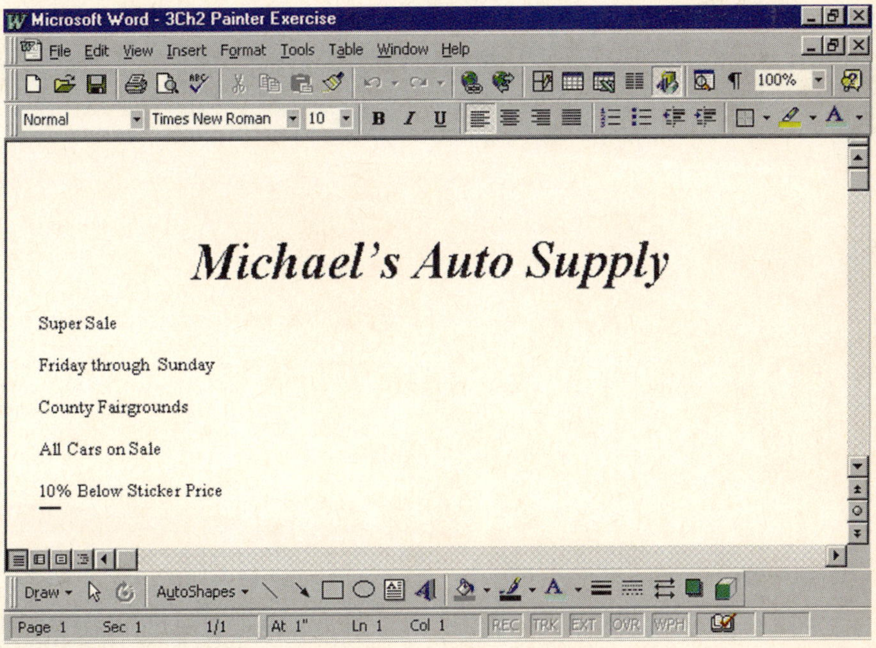

Figure 2.70
The 3Ch2 Painter Exercise document.

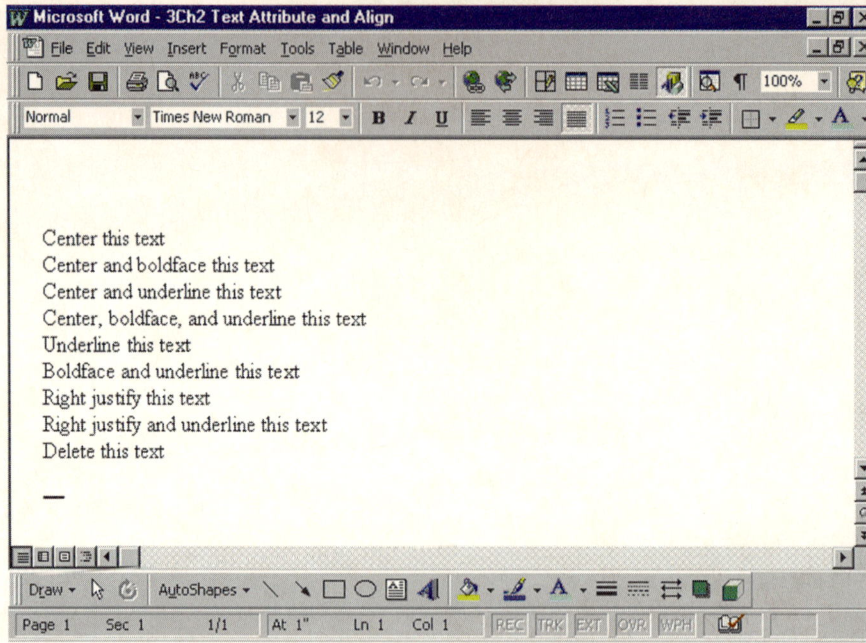

Figure 2.71
The 3Ch2 Text Attribute and Align document.

3. Open the 3Ch2 Font and Attribute Changes document (Figure 2.72). Use selection commands to make the following changes:
   a. For paragraph 1 of page 1, select a different font.
   b. For paragraph 2 of page 1, use italics.
   c. For the first sentence in paragraph 3 of page 1, underline the words.
   d. For paragraph 4 of page 1, choose a larger point size than the default (for example, 16 or 18 points).

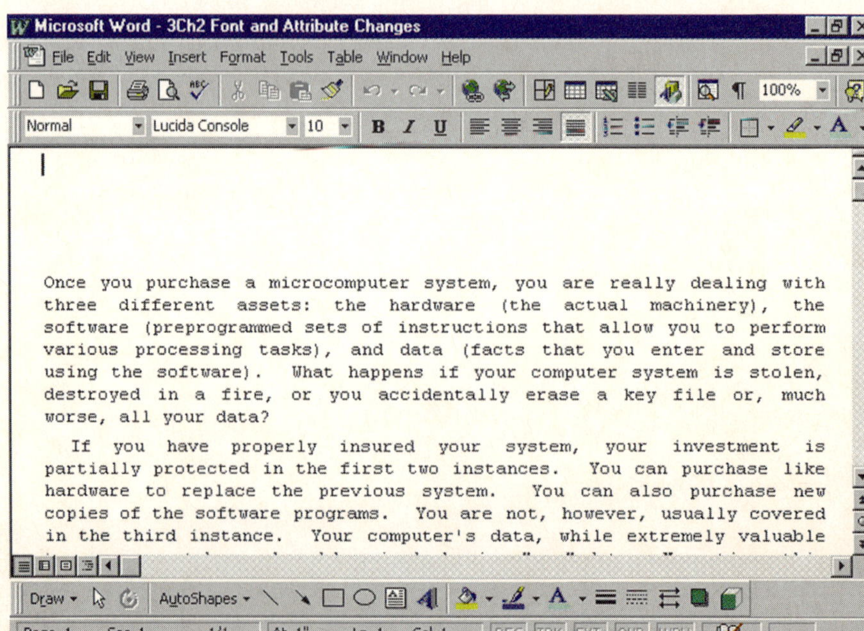

Figure 2.72
The 3Ch2 Font and Attribute Changes document.

e. For the first sentence in paragraph 5 of page 1, use bold.
f. Place your name in the upper-left corner of the document.
g. Print the document.
h. Use the Save As command to save the document using the name M3Ch2 Exercise 3.

4. Clear the screen. Open the M3Ch2 Exercise 3 file.
   a. Change the first three paragraphs to 16 point type.
   b. Change the remaining paragraphs to 18 point type.
   c. Print the document.
   d. Close without saving the document.
5. Clear the screen. Open the 3Ch2 Micros and the Internet document (figure 2.73).
   a. Select the title *Factors Influencing the Growth of Microcomputer Use,* and change it to a different font and larger point size. Also change the title to bold.
   b. Select the five lines under that title, and italicize that text.
   c. Use the same font and point size that you used previously for the heading *Internet Components.*
   d. Italicize the subheads.
   e. Type your name in the upper-left corner of the document.
   f. Use the Save As command to save the document using the name M3Ch2 Exercise 4.
   g. Print the file.
6. Open the 4Ch1 Introduction to Word Processing document. Practice using the various movement commands to move around the document. Close the document without saving any changes.
7. Experiment with using the Office Art feature of Microsoft Office.

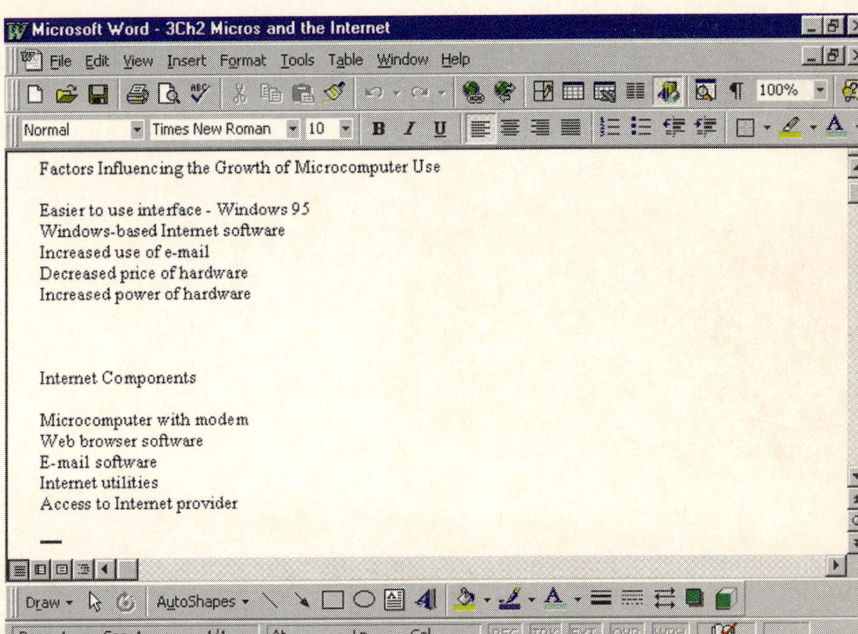

Figure 2.73
The 3Ch2 Micros and the Internet document.

INTERNET EXERCISES

1. Examine a topic that interests you.
   a. Use your browser to visit the Microsoft Web site (http://microsoft. com)
   b. Activate the Personal Computing Web page and then visit the Reference Page. Use the list box to activate the menu of topics available.
   c. Find information about a topic of your choice on this Web page. For instance, the Topics list box provides you with information about purchasing a new car, setting up a family tree, learning to fly, and so forth.
   d. Print one Web page.
2. Get general information about Office 97.
   a. Use your browser to visit the Microsoft Web site (http://microsoft.com).
   b. Click the Products button at the top of the Web page. Once that page is displayed, click the Microsoft Office link.
   c. Now click the link that permits you to examine an overview of Office, learn about new features and examine some case studies. Examine the various links provided on the Web page.
   d. Print one Web page.

Notes

Notes

Notes

Notes

Notes

Notes

Notes

Notes

Notes

Notes

Notes

Notes

OPERATIONS REFERENCE

BUTTON	COMMAND SEQUENCE	KEYS	EXPLANATION
			Opens the Start menu used to start any Office application.
	File, Open	ALT + **F, O**	Opens the Open dialog box used to open a document, search for a document, and view information about a document.
	File, Close	ALT + F12	Closes a document.
	File, Exit	ALT + F4	Exits an application.
	File, New	ALT + **N**	Opens a new document.
	File, Save	SHIFT + F12	Saves a document.
	File, Save As	F12	Saves an unnamed document or saves a document under a new name.
	File, Print	CTRL + SHFT + F12	Prints a document.
	File, Print Preview	ALT + **F, V**	Displays a preview of the document as it will be printed.
	Window	ALT + **W**	Opens the Window menu used to switch among multiple open windows.
	Tools, AutoCorrect		Activates the AutoCorrect feature, which automatically checks the spelling in a document.
	Tools, Spelling	ALT + **T, S**	Opens the Spelling and Grammar dialog box used to check spelling of a document.
		CTRL + **B**	Boldfaces text.
		CTRL + **I**	Italicizes text.
		CTRL + **U**	Underlines text.

BUTTON	COMMAND SEQUENCE	KEYS	EXPLANATION
	Edit, Copy	CTRL + **C**	Copies selected text onto the clipboard.
	Edit, Cut	CTRL + **X**	Cuts selected text from a document and places it on the clipboard.
	Edit, Paste	CTRL + **V**	Takes text from clipboard and puts it in a document at the insertion point.
	Edit, Undo	CTRL + **Z**	Reverses the effect of the last command.
	Edit, Redo	F4	Re-executes the last command.
	Format, Paragraph	CTRL + **L**	Aligns text along the left margin.
	Format, Paragraph	CTRL + **R**	Aligns text along the right margin.
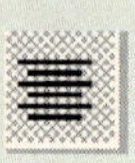	Format, Paragraph	CTRL + **E**	Centers text between the left and right margins.
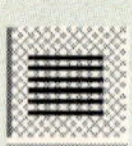	Format, Paragraph	CTRL + **J**	Aligns text along both the left and right margins.
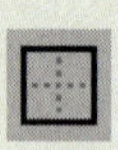	Format, Borders and Shading		Opens the Borders and Shading dialog box used to add borders to selected text or shade selected text.
			Applies all the attributes of selected text to another part of a document.
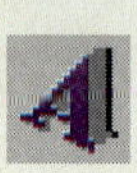	View, Toolbars, Drawing		Activates the Office Art feature used to draw 2-D and 3-D images.

GLOSSARY

AutoCorrect feature Automatically checks for misspelled words and corrects them as you enter text.

binder Holds copies of related electronic documents you have created in various Office applications. You can save, move, and print a binder as you would a single document. Changes that you make to the copy of the document that is in a binder are reflected in the original document.

drag handles Small squares that appear around a selected object in Office Art.

editing A process that can involve correcting misspelled words, inserting new words, and deleting text.

file task buttons Allow you to manipulate files: New, Open, and Save, for example.

font A specific style of type, such as Times Roman, Helvetica, and Courier. Also called a typeface.

font control buttons Allow you to determine the font to use in a document.

Format Painter feature Allows you to apply all the attributes of selected text to another part of a document.

Insert mode Moves existing text in a document to the right when new characters are added. This is the Office default mode.

insertion point The vertical bar that moves as you enter characters, press the arrow keys, or click the mouse.

IntelliMouse A mouse designed by Microsoft to perform a wider variety of functions than a regular mouse. It has a rotating rubber wheel that functions as a control for moving through documents.

Office Art feature Allows you to draw lines, arrows, shapes, shadows, and 3-D images and add them to existing documents.

Office Assistant An Office feature that provides help, solicited and unsolicited. There are several different types of Office Assistant, but all appear as a box in the lower-right corner of the screen.

Overwrite mode Replaces existing characters with characters that you enter from the keyboard. This mode is rarely needed by most users so is not available unless activated at installation.

point The unit of measure of a font. An inch consists of 72 points.

Preview window Displays the document that is active when you issue the Print Preview command.

Print Preview feature Allows you to see what a document will look like before you print it. Accessed by issuing the File, Print Preview command sequence or by clicking the Print Preview button.

shortcut bar A narrow bar that appears above the title bar in some versions of Office. The shortcut bar gives you quick access to applications, documents, the Help system, and CD-ROMs, and it allows you to create new documents quickly.

shortcut icon An icon on the Windows desktop that represents an application.

suite A set of applications designed to work together and share data.

text attribute buttons Allow you to apply boldfacing, italics, and underlining to text as you enter it or to selected text.

Web aware Refers to an application that can be used to access or generate HTML documents. All applications in the Office suite are Web aware.

INDEX